Bill

HOWLER

Ross Malone

ISBN: 978-0-9905974-6-9

Cover Illustration: Katie Blake

Book Layout: Aimee Bachman

Printed in the United States of America

Bluebird Publishing Co.

Dedication

This book is dedicated to my best boyhood friend, David.

We enjoyed great parents, great imaginations, and great adventures.

These places are important in the lives of Billy and me:

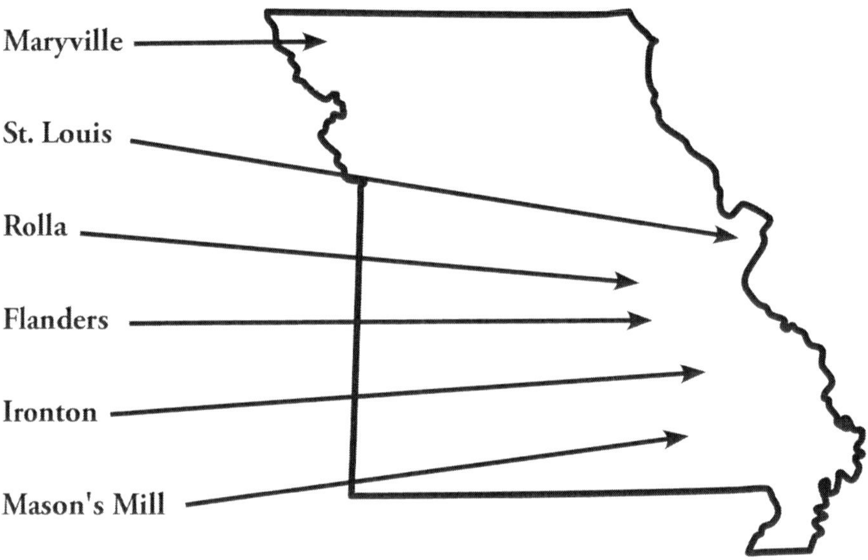

Contents

Meeting Billy Bob Caldwell

It was my very first day at the Morgan Schoolhouse when I met Billy Bob Caldwell. I don't know why, but I liked him instantly and, over the rest of the year, we became good friends. He wasn't like any other kid I ever knew. His dad was a preacher at a little country church and his mom was the school teacher there at Morgan. I soon learned that he was an embarrassment to both of them – at least for a time. They spent their lives telling people to do the right thing and then he became famous for making trouble and telling lies.

We were in the eighth grade and therefore the oldest kids in the little one-room school. When Mrs. Caldwell met me she reminded me that all the other kids looked up to the eighth graders and that it was important for us to set a good example for them. I noticed that she looked over at Billy when she said that. I also saw him turn away from her gaze.

At recess I asked him, "What was that about? You must have done something bad." I was just giving him some friendly teasing but he looked at me with a really serious expression and started to tell me a story that I'll never forget. Over the next couple of days I learned about some things that I thought were just ghost stories or myths but, I have to admit it now, I don't know for sure if they're just stories or maybe they're true.

"I wish I woulda just kept my mouth shut!" Billy told me. "All my life I've been honest and truthful and I always shy away from tellin' lies but now I'm famous in these parts for bein' a liar! Last week I rode with Pap into Flanders to get some groceries and the people was starin' at me. Some of the boys was laughin'. And all I did was tell some folks what I saw that night in the woods."

"I'll tell you just so you'll understand but I swear, if you laugh at me or act like I'm lyin', then I won't be tellin' you the whole story. You might know that we live over by the Current River and that's where I do my fishin' whenever I can. And that's where I saw the Ozark Howler.

"It was gettin' shadowy there in the woods because the sun had just ducked behind the hills and I knew I was gonna have to hurry on up to get home for dinner. It had been a good day at the riverbank and I had a nice string of fish. The ones I kept were all pan-sized and I knew my mom's cornmeal batter would make them perfect. That's what I was thinking about as I followed the path up across Chiggerchaw Ridge and back toward our place. Since my mind was on fried fish I wasn't paying much attention to anything else so what happened next is a little foggy in my mind.

"Picture this. It was getting dark in the deep woods and I was dodging blackberry stickers and thinking about food when I thought I heard a twig snap right behind me. I looked back and didn't see anything so I just kept on down the little path. When I heard the growl – that's when I knew somethin' was really up!"

He had me hooked with his story now. "What growled? Was it really a howler?" I asked.

"Well now, there's the problem," he answered. "I can tell you what I think and what I saw but people are all gonna be tellin' you that I was wrong. One thing I do believe is that it was my string of fish that started the trouble. I think the beast could smell the fish and thought I was invintin' him for a feast. I was just afraid I might be the desert so I started movin' a lot faster and as it was getting darker, and I was goin' faster, I started trippin' over roots and runnin' into low-hangin' branches and pretty soon I was all worked up. I was almost to the point of runnin' but then I stopped dead in my tracks.

"Standin' there in the path right in front of me was what looked like a cat but it was bigger than any cat. It was bigger than any dog! It was about the size of a really good buck! Now you gotta remember that it was almost dark so I couldn't see too clear but I know it had long shaggy fur like a bear and I think its fur was black but I can't be certain. And he was stocky and powerful-built like a bear too.

"He just stood there lookin' at me and at my fish and at my pole. Maybe he thought I might be able to hit him or stick him with a fishin' pole, I don't know. But he just stood there for a minute with drool comin' outa his mouth and breathin' real heavy. Then he took a step towards me. I threw the whole string of fish at him and started runnin' off toward the right. I took a shortcut home that night right through a giant patch of wild blackberry brambles and cut up my feet and tore my shirt but I got away.

"I was still runnin' as hard as I could when I heard somethin' I aint never heard before or since. I heard a sudden, bone-chillin', go-home-and-change-your-underwear kind of a howl! It came from back where the big cat was. But you know that cats don't howl and neither do bears for that matter. That's why I think it was what the old-timers call the Ozark Howler."

I told Billy Bob, "I always lived in the city so I don't know about these kinds of things but I used to hear about a Devil Cat. Do you think that's what you saw?"

"That's right," Billy answered. "Devil Cats and Ozark Howlers are the same thing. But they call 'em Devil Cats because of the horns on their heads and I didn't see any horns at all. Remember now, it was pretty dark so I can't be certain but all I really saw was two ears stickin' up above that awful face."

Mrs. Caldwell rang the school bell and we had to go back inside for reading and ciphering classes but I knew that I wanted to hear more about that night when Billy Bob met the creature in his woods.

Climb a Tree to Tell a Lie

There's a saying in the Ozarks, "Some folks will climb a tree to tell a lie when truth would do on the ground." I learned the wisdom of that saying over the years. It seems like people, especially politicians, seem to enjoy putting one over on us. They will go out of their way and go to extra trouble just to see if they can get a big one past us. Politicians like to call their lies "spin" but it really doesn't change the fact that what they're saying just isn't completely true.

Living in the woods or in the city either one, it's a good thing to recognize lies when you hear them. Wise people are always on the lookout for people who lie. We get suspicious of our neighbors because of it.

Here's where I think I understand a part of the story that many people don't. Some of those suspicious people want to show how smart they are by catching someone else in a lie. Sometimes they should be a little more trusting and listen to what people are telling them.

Billy Bob's parents didn't understand why his feet and ankles were all cut up after running through the brambles. They were upset about his shirt being ripped. They were angry and that made it easy for them to think that he was making up a story to keep out of trouble. He was telling them that he was running in a panic and that they would have been running too. They became more and more angry with him and told him to, "Just stop the fantastic stories and tell us the truth!" To this day I don't think his own parents believe him.

Billy's parents hadn't seen anything yet. He was hoping that someone would believe him. He was especially hoping that someone else would see the Howler and verify his story. Then his parents would feel bad about not believing him and treat him even better than before. He felt certain that, if someone else would see the Howler, Billy would be recognized as a long-suffering and pitiable hero. That's why he told the newspaper editor about the creature.

Now small town newspaper editors are always looking for a good story with local interest. That's exactly what Billy brought in that morning. He had asked to go along when his father left to visit some sick folks in Flanders and, while he waited, Billy went over to the office of the Flanders Weekly. He found the editor, Mr. Bradley, and his assistant setting type for the next edition and asked if he could tell them about something he saw.

"Son," Mr. Bradley said, "were right in the middle of this and I can't let myself be distracted. Can you tell me about it quickly?"

"Well, sir, I saw an Ozark Howler out by my house and the Current River," Billy stated calmly.

"Aren't you the Caldwell boy?" the editor wanted to know.

On hearing that Billy was, in fact, the person the editor thought, Mr. Bradley smiled at his assistant and invited Billy to join him at his desk. As I said before, newspaper editors are always watching for interesting stories with a local flavor and this one had promise. Not only did it involve a monster in the dark woods, but the witness was the son of a respected minister and a popular and pretty school teacher. Perfect!

"Start at the beginning," Mr. Bradley invited. "Tell me all about it."

****

No one knew about Billy Bob's visit to the newspaper office until Friday when the story was published. Billy's family lived way out in the country so they didn't know anything about it until church on Sunday morning. Usually when the Caldwell family arrives they are the first people there. This morning they were almost the last. In fact, by the time they arrived, there were so many people that Mr. Caldwell figured there were more people there on that ordinary day than on Easter Sunday! He suspected that this was not an ordinary Sunday at all – and he was right.

For a time, everything seemed fine. With all those people there, the hymns were loud and spirited. The sermon was "Mountain Top Moments" about seeing God's work in nature all around us. People listened very carefully to every word. With so many people in the church the collection basket was heavy with nickels and dimes and that was good and, sadly, unusual. After the church service was finished people seemed reluctant to leave and seemed to want to stay in their seats.

Rev. Caldwell thought to himself, "My sermons usually have people wanting to get out the door as fast as possible. Something's wrong." That's when he made his big mistake.

"There's something different about this morning," he said. "Is there something I should know? Is there something we need to talk about?"

One of the Church Deacons stood and said, "Brother Caldwell, what's all this about Satan's creatures roaming our woods? Are you claiming to have seen the Ozark Howler too?"

Nothing is the Same

You know how a good meal takes longer to eat than an ordinary one, don't you? Some of the food is just so juicy and good that you want to chew on it and get at all of the flavor. You hate to see a good meal come to an end. Well in our Ozark hills, life is usually pretty quiet and folks like it that way. But sometimes something comes along that's so good you just want to make it last. You want to chew on it and get at all the flavor that's there. And you're always hoping that there will be something sweet at the end just to top it all off. That's just the way people treated Billy Bob's story.

It all started that morning at the church with everyone watching the Reverend Mr. Caldwell sweat and squirm and stutter. That gave them something to talk about all the way home. Then, as they told their friends, the description of the minister's suffering grew and Reverend Caldwell became the most ridiculed man in the area.

Mrs. Caldwell didn't come out too well either. People began to say things like, "Wouldn't you think a school teacher could control her son better than that?"

No matter how the conversation began, it always turned toward Billy Bob. He became the "bad example" that every parent used for warning their children about things like lying and about, "letting your imagination run away with you." It wasn't long before people began to tell their children about other bad things – things that Billy Bob never actually did.

"Don't let yourself get to be like that wild Caldwell boy!" they would say. That would always be followed by some accusation like "He chews gum you know." They warned their children that the villainous Billy Bob did unforgivable sins like smoking grape vines, peeking into the girl's coatroom at school, and skinny dipping in the Current River.

The bottom line was that the local girls didn't know what to think because Billy never seemed to be such a bad kid. To the boys on the other hand, Billy Bob Caldwell became a local legend – a greatly admired hero. They saw him as their own version of Tom Sawyer or Huckleberry Finn. He was the only boy brave enough to do all the social evils that their parents warned them about. More than that, he broke the rules when his father was a preacher and his mother was a teacher. Most important, he had stood face-to-face with the horrible Ozark Howler and lived to tell about it!

I said that things started that morning at church but that certainly wasn't the end of the problems. The sheriff sent his deputy to take an account of what had been seen. He said that the law required them to make a note of anything unusual or suspicious and an Ozark Howler was both. The report was filed and the sighting became an official legal happening.

People began to stop Billy's parents whenever they saw them. They all wanted to complain about, "...what that boy has caused." They said their children wouldn't go into the woods now to hunt mushrooms, check the rabbit traps, gather nuts, pick blackberries, or anything else.

The newspaper office and the library were flooded with questions about what Ozark Howlers eat. "Are my chickens safe? How about our cats and dogs? Will the thing kill a calf or a pig? Is it big enough to attack a cow, or a horse, or a mule? How fast do they run?" That last question was the key to what everyone really wanted to know. "Do Howlers eat people?"

You see, the very people who were the first to yell and accuse Billy Bob of lying were also the very first ones to begin believing his story. The men started keeping their hunting rifles with them at all times. They might tell you they were hunting but they never came home with any deer or turkeys. They were really just afraid of the Howler!

Someone said that, in all of recorded history, there had never been a case of an Ozark Howler attacking a group of people. So the women began to go out only in groups and they quit sending children on errands unless they went with a herd of other children. Dent County began to look like a military base with all of the weapons that the men carried and all of the squads and platoons of people hurrying from here to there.

One man who had been on a business trip came home and noticed that when people greeted him they all had nervous little smiles and their eyes darted here and there as they talked. "Really strange," he thought. He left the town thinking that he knew it well but when he came back it was definitely different than before.

Billy Bob's parents told each other that they must be strong. They assured each other that this would all just go away and they could get back to normal. "After all," they said, "it couldn't get any worse." They had no idea!

The Snowball Effect

It was all very interesting while it was happening right there in Flanders and in the communities around the town. But, just like poison ivy, it got out of control and grew and grew and grew.

Did you ever stop and think about how people like to be scared? That's why we pay to ride roller coasters. It's why we jump out and startle our friends. We love to hear spooky stories around a campfire and we pay to watch scary movies. It's fun to be scared! The people around Flanders were having fun feeling threatened by a creature in the deep woods. Editor Bradley knew that when he stopped what he was doing to write down Billy Bob's story.

What no one yet realized was that people in other places enjoy being scared too. And it's really easy to have fun being scared when it's someone else who has to deal with the monsters. As soon as The Flanders Weekly newspaper published its story, the people around Flanders knew about the Ozark Howler. But newspaper reporters and editors read what happens in other newspapers also. Billy Bob's neighbors began to realize this when the first automobile arrived from Rolla. A reporter wanted to know all the details about what had happened for his newspaper in Rolla.

They definitely knew that trouble was on its way when, the next day, a reporter stepped off the train. That man was from St. Louis but the very next day reporters arrived from Springfield, Jefferson City, and Columbia. Automobiles brought newspaper reporters from Lebanon, Cape Girardeau, and Poplar Bluff.

At first Billy Bob liked the idea because he thought more people would know about the Howler and be on the watch for it. Just as soon as one or two more people reported seeing the beast, he would be vindicated and would achieve the status of a local hero. He gladly told them everything he knew and everything he thought might be interesting or helpful. His parents were not so eager or willing to speak to the press.

One day Orville Wellman, the Mayor of Flanders came out to Billy's country home. "Do you understand that we're trying to attract a new mill to locate in our town? They'll produce barrel staves." he said. "Do you understand that it would bring about thirty new jobs and even more work for the lumberjacks? But no one is going to want to work cutting trees if there is a bloodthirsty animal lurking in the woods! No one wants to move their family into some nice little home so they can be visited at night by a monster! Your boy is killing our town!"

In spite of the Mayor's pleading, the story didn't go away. Bittersweet Magazine came to do in depth stories about the people, the location, and the local opinions. National Geographic filled the forests with cameras. Each camera was attached to a fish lying on the ground so that when the Howler picked up the fish, the camera in the tree would snap a picture.

Billy Bob showed them where to put the cameras and the fish. He showed them where he was when he first heard the twig snap, where he saw the creature, and where he was when he heard the howl. Of course they put cameras all along he banks of the Current River in case the Howler came to fish or get a drink.

****

As it turned out, the cameras produced no pictures at all. The young reporters from Bittersweet could find no tracks for any large cat-type animal. People began to doubt the existence of the Ozark Howler. People began to think of Billy as a liar. The Mayor encouraged them to think that because he was convinced that the presence of a Howler was bad for business.

Then Able Finch came to the newspaper office saying that one of his calves was missing and that his dog had died mysteriously. "It's very strange," he said.

Then another farmer told the editor that three of his piglets had been carried off the previous week. "There were tracks about the size of a bobcat's," he said. "But I suppose the tracks could have been made by baby Howlers."

"OH NO!" people began to say. "We thought there might be one Howler but now we hear that there may be more!"

"It only makes sense," others would wisely say. "If there's one, it only makes sense that there could be more."

The Mayor still wanted to convince everyone that there was no monster in the woods so he came up with a story blaming Billy Bob. "Don't you see?" the Mayor asked. "That boy got himself caught in a big fat lie so now he's started hiding calves and taking piglets and making trouble so people will blame it all on some ridiculous beast! I'm not saying that he's a thief. I'm just saying that he's desperate to get himself out of this trouble."

People began to look at Billy suspiciously again until a farmer over in Phelps County told people that his wife had disappeared and he blamed it on the Ozark Howler. People who knew him said he was the meanest man in the county and that his wife had just jumped on a train in Rolla and left him. But it was still enough of a story that people once more wondered if it might be the creature.

"How many might there be?" they would ask. Or "How far do they roam? How big is their range?"

Then two young boys walking home from their aunt's house near Steeleville said that they heard a howling in the woods and it didn't sound like anything they had ever heard before. "Of course we didn't see him!" they told everyone. "We were running as fast as we could!"

Fame & Notoriety

There were some People who actually liked the threat of a monster in the woods. The station master at the railroad said that all of the reporters were bringing a brisk business to the depot. The Two Sisters Café put a sign in the window saying they had a new sandwich called the Big Cat Special. The sign said it was "Howling Good." The boarding house was so full that two other families started taking in boarders.

Two no-account men borrowed a horse and carriage and began to hang out around the railroad station offering to take tourists on a tour of "Howler Country." This didn't really hurt anyone except Billy Bob's family. You see, sometimes they would be doing all the things people do when they live way out in the country and then they would look up to see several people watching them. Billy's mother especially hated this.

Billy had a different attitude and he would smile and strut and make a big show out of mucking the garden, fetching water, or even going to the outhouse. Sometimes he would even go up and talk to the tourists and sign autographs. One couple owned a camera and they paid him five cents to pose for a picture. That's when Billy's parents stepped in and told him he couldn't do business with the tourists any more. You see, they still thought he was lying. Or, as they put it, "His imagination has gotten away from him."

Billy told me that his own personal favorite thing that happened involved Mary Jean McBride. Everyone agreed that she was the most beautiful girl in the high school and she came to Billy Bob with an idea to get rich. She was a good artist and she offered to draw a picture of the

Ozark Howler based on Billy Bob's description. This required Billy to sit with her for hours and talk softly about the details of the creature and the subtle variations of her art. He told me that Mary Jean was his first true love. He said he couldn't expect her to like him in the same way though because she was a year older and in high school already.

It turns out that she was also a talented artist and she had a gift for sales and marketing. She got Mr. Bradley at the newspaper office to print copies of the finished drawing and she began to sell them for five cents each. She sold the same thing but autographed by Billy Bob for eight cents. People could buy them in the general store but even more people wanted to buy them from the pretty local girl who was selling them at the railroad depot.

Soon Billy began to go to town every Saturday morning and pose with the tourists while having their photographs made. For fifteen cents they got a photograph, a printed picture of the Howler, and it was even signed by Billy Bob himself. With Mary Jean and Billy Bob each getting half of everything they sold, they were soon accumulating a good deal of money. Even Billy's parents began to recognize the good in that and his father encouraged Billy's entrepreneurial spirit. His mother still suspected that he just wanted to hang out with Mary Jean.

****

Then, one day in late August, a man named Arlo Huntley came to town. No one knew who he was back then but of course you recognize his name as the famous bluegrass musician. He stepped down from the train with a tiny suitcase in one hand and a guitar case in the other. He looked around and went over to the Two Sisters Café where he ordered black coffee and hot apple pie with a slice of cheese on the top.

Arlo Huntley was soft-spoken and polite and people were happy to talk to such a pleasant stranger. They told him the big news about Billy Bob and the Ozark Howler. One man went next door and borrowed a picture of the beast. They told him about all of the reporters and about the letters that had been arriving from Boston, and San Francisco, and even London, England.

Arlo listened to every word. He seemed to be truly interested and he was. His expression was calm but his mind was racing with new ideas. By noon he had disappeared into the woods outside of town where he sat on the grass leaning against a tree and composing a song. By four o'clock he had found his way to the Caldwell home and asked to speak with the family. They liked the quiet man with the good manners and welcomed him in. For some reason, they trusted him.

He talked with Billy and his parents for about an hour and was gone. Someone said he thought Arlo got on the train the next morning but no one knows for sure. Someone said he stayed out in the woods for a few nights hoping to meet up with the creature. At any rate, no one really knows just how long he stayed or when he left. No one thought any more about him until a gramophone record arrived at the general store with a recording of "Arlo Huntley's newest musical sensation – The Ballad of Billy & the Howler."

Mr. Jensen who owned the store put the record on the gramophone and listened to it with the other people who were in the store at the time.

This is what they heard:

The Ballad of Billy & the Howler

Billy Bob was a comin' home,
And it was dark out in the wood.
He had fish swingin' on a string
When somethin' froze him where he stood.

A howlin' and a screamin',
Like the Devil's own voice he heard.
He commenced to movin' toward
His house and sayin' not a word.

Then the creature showed himself.
An Ozark Howler sure!
But Billy wasn't scared, no sir!
He used those fish as a lure.

He threw the fish at the awful cat,
And skedaddled on from there.
The howler felt himself content,
To dine without a care.

He didn't know who he'd encountered
Out in that dark wood.
Billy Bob made up his mind
To catch him if he could.

For two long days he chased that beast,
But the cat stayed just ahead.
Billy showed determination,
The Howler was filled with dread.

Alas, there are no Howlers now,
Near Flanders' whereabouts.
They've gone away now,
You can have no doubts.

You can still find them in Missouri,
Arkansas and Illinois.
But none will come near Flanders,
Thanks to one courageous boy.

Billy Bob Caldwell, you're a hero true.
Billy Bob, Billy Bob. What will we do?
When confronted by our demons,
Will we be as brave as you?
Will we be as brave as you?

In the ladies' fine parlors, in grange halls, and in saloons everywhere people were soon singing the praises of the courageous Billy Bob Caldwell. Some people had electricity and some of them had radios so they heard Arlo Huntley singing the song in their own living rooms and kitchens. People began to swarm into Flanders to see the brave people in town who had lived with a monster nearby. They especially wanted to catch a glimpse of the courageous young man who "...gave the creature what for!"

Finally the merchants convinced the Mayor to get on the band wagon and welcome the new flood of money into the town. Everyone got together to plan a big celebration called "Howler Day" and they decided to advertise it in newspapers all across the Midwest. They promised the Mayor that he could make a speech if he would let Billy Bob tell the crowds his version of the story.

Billy's parents weren't so happy about the idea but then the Howler Day Committee told Billy's father that he could lead the opening prayer for the festivities and that it would be a good chance for him to reach out to some of the squirrel turners, moon shiners, and ruffians who lived in the county. He reluctantly agreed and a new tradition was born in the forested hills of the Ozarks.

Ozark Howler Day

People usually like the idea of a big party and, from the very beginning, Howler Days grabbed everyone's imaginations. They chose a shady spot between the bank and the general store and said that the Brass Band could perform there. Right in front of that they decided to erect a small speaker's stand. Then the band director invited some of his friends from other towns to play and instead of seven people in the band, they realized there would be fifteen that day. So a new place was chosen on a vacant lot. Some men decided that they would build a band stand large enough for a fifteen-piece band and the speakers could speak from there. That's how Flanders got its very first bandstand.

At Madison's Stable which was now also a Ford dealer, Mr. Madison's son got an idea to raffle off a new automobile. A new Ford sold for about $300 in those days so they only needed to get 300 people to buy a one dollar ticket and the Madisons would make a little profit. It turned out that 324 people bought tickets and some people bought more than one. The Madisons would never tell how much profit they made but it must have been nearly $100.00!

The smartest people of all seemed to be three women. Margie and Maggie from the Two Sisters Café hired a man to build several picnic tables and put them in the shade next to the café. Each table was covered with a bright red and white table cloth and looked very festive. These tables allowed them to serve more than twice as many customers as normal. Everyone discovered that they enjoyed eating outside and the picnic tables remained for many years and were enjoyed by many people.

The other bright woman was Mary Jean McBride. She got her uncle's Bakers Tent and erected it near the new bandstand. She was careful to put up her tent before anyone else and therefore got the best spot for her business. "Location is very important," she told Billy.

On the big day she and Billy Bob put up the flap and sat inside the spacious tent and she sold pictures while Billy autographed them. On the walls of the tent she hung other artwork that she had created and made a nice profit on those also.

On the morning of the big day, Flanders's Main Street was crowded with carriages, wagons, and automobiles carrying people and the supplies they would need for their little booths. By nine o'clock the street was lined on both sides with tents, lean-tos, and canopies each sheltering someone else with something else to sell or have done.

One old man had whittled puzzles, animals, and all sorts of things out of pine wood. Many women were there selling pies and cookies and sandwiches of every description. Women sold hand-made baskets and hand-woven capes and shawls. Some booths sold kettle beef or venison stew.

At another booth they were actually cooking fresh catfish while the customers waited. After it cooled the people could dip the pieces of fish into a sauce and eat it with their fingers. It seemed slightly naughty to be eating food with your fingers but everyone got into the spirit and enjoyed it.

By noon the Brass Band had assembled and was playing. Some people began to dance right on the street in front of the band. When the band finished, the town's Mayor was introduced and he asked everyone to bow their heads as Reverend Caldwell asked the Lord to bless the day's activities. Then Mayor Wellman gave his speech and seemed somewhat annoyed that so many people were not listening. Finally he introduced

Billy Bob and the crowd returned to the band stand. There was no one left at the booths or in the café or in the store. Everyone came to hear what Billy had to say. After all he was the hero of the ballad and the reason that the townspeople were here to celebrate.

****

I hadn't thought much about Billy's speech but, of course, he had. It was important for him to sound like a nice honest boy who just told what he really saw. He didn't want anyone to ever again think that he was lying, steeling pigs and cows, or any of the other things that people claimed he did. He had carefully planned every detail of what he would say and how he would say it.

"When I was walking home . . ." he said softly.

"Speak up, boy! We can't hear you!" someone shouted. Several people put their hands up to there ears to signal Billy and others yelled, "Louder!"

Billy started again. "I'm not used to all the attention," Billy told them. "I'm just a regular kid who saw something and told people about it. I'm just not comfortable talking to everyone about it. I suppose you'd say I'm shy."

Some of us knew that Billy Bob Caldwell had never been shy. But he convinced a lot of people that he was. "What a sweet boy," one woman said.

"When I was walking home," Billy said much louder this time, "I was carrying a string of fish and I guess the smell of those critters just drew that big cat thing in my direction. You know how cats are about fish."

Everyone's heads bobbed up and down in agreement. "Yes, sir," they thought, "this boy knows what he's talking about. It's true that cats are drawn to the smell of fish." Billy had them hooked.

When he hooked those fish, he pulled them in and strung 'em up. When he hooked the folks in that crowd, he literally pulled them in too. Without even realizing it, they silently moved forward to get closer to the fourteen-year-old American hero to hear every word he said and every breath he took. He landed them hook, line, and sinker.

He told the story of meeting the Ozark Howler and, before anyone could ask any questions, he moved right on to meeting Arlo Huntley and told the crowd about what a nice guy the now-famous singer really was. He also told the crowd that there was a talented artist in town and that he would be in her tent signing autographs and that everyone was invited. Then, before anyone could ask any questions, he left the band stand and hustled over to Mary Jean's tent while the people applauded loudly. It was over and decided. No one could prove that he was a liar and no one could doubt that he was a hero. I had to admit that he was amazing!

A group of string musicians replaced Billy on the stage and they picked, strummed, and fiddled the happiest music outside of Heaven. Now different people were dancing. The dances now weren't as elegant as before but they were every bit as much fun.

I would like to tell you that the rest of the day was happy and delightful and full of sunshine and peppermint sticks but that wouldn't be true. There was still one more big event planned for Howler Day.

****

A group of boys from Eldridge School had a sinister idea of how this day was going to go. They were tired of hearing about this hero kid and they were going to make news in a very different way. Back behind the bank they had parked a wagon loaded with wooden boxes. Slowly and quietly the boys meandered along in front of the bank and then quietly moved back to the rear of the building.

They placed three long boards on the back of the wagon and let one end of each rest on the ground below. Then they sprinkled a few little chunks of cheese and some earthworms on the wagon floor between the boxes. Then some more cheese and worms on the boards leading down to the ground. Finally they opened the boxes and let the skunks out.

The little critters quickly came out of the boxes and began looking for the cheese they had smelled. Then they followed the trail down the planks eating as they went. Once on the ground they began to explore in hopes of finding even more of their favorite treats. They waddled out into Main Street and weren't even noticed at first.

It was a little boy about four years old who noticed them first. He said, "Look, mommy! Kitties!" He made a dash to hold and pet one of the kitties and his mother turned to see what was happening. She became the first woman to scream that day.

Everyone turned and, as soon as they figured out what was happening, they also began to yell, give orders, and especially to run. This all made the skunks very apprehensive and they turned toward the nearest people and stood with their tails erect and their backsides in firing position.

One of the skunks must have given the command because, all at once, they began to spray Main Street and all its inhabitants. Two small children just sat down and cried when they got sprayed. This caused their parents to have to run back into the line of fire to get the children. They paid the penalty and smelled for days afterwards.

As people ran screaming they alarmed even more people who stepped from the places where they had been to see what was happening. They stepped into the middle of a stampede and were knocked on their keisters. They immediately scrambled back to their feet as the black and white army spread out through the middle of town.

Some people stampeded through the tent poles and brace ropes which caused the tents and canopies to topple. Several lean-tos fell but luckily no one was injured. The diners at the picnic tables by Two Sisters Café grabbed their children and fled. But they were soon replaced by other diners – black and white ones who smelled the good food and got up on the tables to help themselves.

Two of the tents that came down knocked over cooking kettles as they fell. This left kettle beef and catfish spread out as a feast for the uninvited guests. In time, the skunks had their fill and stopped eating. However they had no intention of leaving all this good food so they just settled down and lounged around in the late afternoon sun.

Some townspeople tried to scare them away by sicking their dogs on the critters but the dogs were too smart. They stood and whined and looked up at their masters. But not one of them would go after the skunks.

Finally the sun set and with the dusk the skunks began to think of where they might settle for the night. They nibbled a few last bites and then waddled out of town into the surrounding countryside.

Slowly, by lantern light, the people came back to clean up and pick up. There was a good deal of money in boxes under the fallen tents, canopies, and lean-tos. As they worked, people began to poke fun at each other and laugh. Everyone was accused of being the fastest runner, or the smelliest man, or questioned about why he or she was afraid of such small animals. Everyone laughed together when someone recalled the little boy who started it all by saying, "Look, Mommy. Kitties!"

As people worked and laughed in the lantern light, the musicians came back and began to play. People sang the familiar songs and cleaned and laughed some more. People from all over went home that day with a wonderful story to tell.

"Those people in Flanders really know how to throw a party!" they would say. Or, "Even when things were about as bad as you could imagine, those people in Flanders found a way to sing and laugh about it. Flanders sure is a nice little town!"

Tigers, and Dogs, and...Howlers

This was the time in our history when schools began to choose names for their teams. Professional teams already had names like the St. Louis Cardinals and Browns. Kansas City had the Blues and Monarchs and other small town teams had names too. Next the colleges named their teams and it was just natural then for the high school teams to do the same.

So instead of saying the Rolla High School basketball team people referred to them as the Rolla Bull Dogs. Lebanon High School's teams had become the Yellowjackets. At Aurora, their teams were the Houn' Dawgs and Flanders High School's teams were called the Tigers.

Hendron was a small community east of Flanders and the folks at several small country schools around Hendron decided that they would form a new High School for their students who had graduated from the eight grade. And, you guessed it. The sports teams at Hendron High wanted a name too so the students voted to be the Hendron Howlers. Since no one had ever been hurt by a Howler, and people were having lots of fun with the Howler stories and sightings, the Howler became quite a poplular creature.

And speaking of sightings, people began to blame everything that couldn't be easily explained on the Howlers. They also brought their stories to the newspaper so the stories could be shared with the rest of the community. More and more people began to buy the newspapers so the editor encouraged everyone to tell him such stories.

Able Cranston told that his family had been frightened on Wednesday night by what sounded like something big up on their roof.

Some neighbors pointed out that Wednesday had been very windy and that Able had big tree branches above his roof. Then they would always add, "But you never know!"

Marie Oswald reported that both of her cows had mysteriously stopped giving milk. People read about it and said, "Lots of things can cause cows to go dry. But you never know!"

Usually when horses were missing the sheriff would organize a posse and they would fan out looking for clues and try to find the horse thieves. But when Norm Howsert's team of prize-winning draft horses both disappeared, no one wanted to go into the woods looking for the culprits. "What if it was the Ozark Howler?" they asked. "I don't want to run into him out there!"

"But how could the Howler take two big horses at the same time?" the sheriff wanted to know. No one could answer him or argue with him – they just didn't go into the woods.

On the other hand, while some men wouldn't go near the woods, "hunters" began to spend more time in the woods. They claimed to be looking for the Howler but they often returned to their homes in the morning with headaches, like they had been drinking. They said, "Well, maybe just a little," but mostly they seemed to be sitting around a campfire with lots of their friends and having a good time.

Of course horses weren't the only animals that went missing. All sorts of pets and livestock disappeared and the Howler was always suspected "Because you never know." It's interesting too that when they disappeared the event was reported to the newspaper. When some were eventually found, that was never reported.

One man who had been gambling came home with no money left. He told his wife that he had stopped to rest in the woods and started to count his money when the Howler approached and scared him so badly that he ran away leaving the money behind. He couldn't remember exactly where he left the money so he couldn't get it back. His two children did their civic duty and reported the event to the newspaper.

As these reports kept coming in, one of the Rolla newspaper reporters made a careful list and found that, at that point in time, Howler sightings or Howler suspicions had been reported in twenty-one Missouri counties plus two in Arkansas and three in Illinois. Even with all of the widespread "sightings" people still remembered that it all started in the woods near Flanders. That's why someone finally convinced the Mayor that it was their claim to fame.

That's also why one Monday morning the residents found nicely painted signs on each of the four roads leading into town that said, "Howler Country." That same morning someone placed a large sign on the lawn in front of the County Courthouse that said "Flanders, the Capital of Howler Country." The Ozark Howler episode, which had started out with people saying it was the outrageous lie of a schoolboy, had become very official and the local merchants, and city government, and the county government all seemed to be going along with it.

Saved by the Howler

One Friday night a horseback rider came to Billy's house. It was a young boy who asked if his father could come to Flanders. A lady from Rev. Caldwell's church was very ill and expected to die. She wanted to talk with her minister before she passed away. Billy's father asked Billy if he would like to ride along. "It may be late when we come home," he said, "and it would be good to have you along to talk so I don't fall asleep while I drive." Billy quickly agreed to ride along.

While his father spoke with the dying lady, Billy walked around town. He had never seen Flanders this way before. Living in the country, he only came to town when there was shopping or some other business to be done. But now all of the stores were closed. Some street lamps were lit along the two main streets but the rest of the town was dark (and a little scary). Billy liked that.

He decided to get away from the main street and walk in the alley behind the stores and the bank and the café. As he walked, he startled a cat and it screeched and jumped from a box it was in. As the box fell and the cat screeched in the dark, Billy Bob's heart jumped and he caught his breath. "Wow!" he thought. "That scared me to death. I'm glad I came back here.

Then he looked to see where the cat had jumped to and he noticed something odd. It had jumped right through an open window. He wondered why a window would be open on such a chilly night. He recognized it as the back window of the general store so, being helpful, he decided to close the window for them. First however, he looked inside to see if he could get the cat to come back out. He leaned through the window looked all around in the dark and said, "I know you're in here. Come on now, show yourself."

That's when a big set of hands grabbed him by the back of his jacket and the back of his pants, pulled him through the window and threw him on the floor. There in the dark Billy could feel something wet and knew that his forehead and his left cheek were bleeding. They were both sore from scraping on the wooden floor when he hit.

In the darkness he heard one man's voice say, "He said he knew we were in here. I had to nab him."

Another man answered, "I know. I know. But this messes everything up. The best thing we can do is to finish our job and get outta here. Tie him up and stuff him in one of those empty barrels."

As Billy was being tied with a rope, his eyes began to adjust to the darkness and he could see the shapes of three men moving around. One seemed to be the boss and was barking orders to the other two. When he was tied, two of the men picked Billy up and put him into the top of a big open barrel sitting with several others there in the back room. As he stood there in the barrel, he couldn't move his hands which were tied behind him and he couldn't move his feet because they were confined in the barrel. He started to say something but just then one of the men stuffed a piece of cloth into his mouth.

Billy gave up and just let his legs fold as he collapsed down into the barrel. A good deal of time went by and the man who seemed to be the leader said, "That's all of it. Get your stuff and don't leave anything behind. We gotta go."

"What about the kid?" one man asked.

"He saw us all," the leader said. "We can't leave someone behind to identify us. We'll have to get rid of him."

Just then Billy heard someone outside calling his name. It was his dad! "Billy! Billy! Where are you?"

Billy tried to yell a reply but he could only get the cloth out of one corner of his mouth. He started yelling through the little opening. As the strange sounds echoed around inside the big barrel, it must have sounded even more strange. But it was enough and his father heard him.

Since his father was in the back of the store, the three burglars ran out the front and disappeared. Rev. Caldwell climbed in through the open window and found Billy tied up there in a barrel in the dark. "What on earth happened?" he wanted to know. Billy quickly told him the story and they ran to wake the sheriff.

The sheriff sent Billy one way and his father in a different direction to gather the deputies and some other men to track down the burglars. "If they are trying to get to a town, they just about have to go north toward Rolla," the sheriff told the men. "If they are trying to get into the woods and hide, south would be the best way. If they go east they'll be stopped by the river and the ferry boat isn't running at night so they won't go that way." So he sent two men west and then several men to the north and several more men to the south.

Soon fresh horse tracks were found going south from town and into the wilderness. The deputy pointed out how deep some of the tracks were. "These horses are loaded with something heavy," he said. Soon three men were found with three packhorses loaded with silver dinner ware that they were planning to melt down to sell for the precious metal. They also had a large number of pocket watches and knives that could be easily sold.

There was no doubt that these were the men. "Tie their hands behind their backs and put 'em up on the horses," the deputy ordered. Soon all three of the strangers were in the county jail and Billy was a hero again!

****

A funny thing happened when the story appeared in the next newspaper. Mr. Bradley, the editor, told what had happened including the part about Billy down inside the barrel yelling and the sound echoing around. The article said, "The thieves must have thought the Howler was there in the store with them!" Of course he was joking but people took it seriously and began to talk about how this brilliant young man had tricked the burglars. Now he was an even bigger hero.

With that sort of a twist on the story, Billy was in the newspapers again and the story was being read all over the Midwest and even farther away. They all said that the thieves were afraid of the Ozark Howler but Billy wasn't. They all said that this young genius had just outsmarted the villains. People started buying and singing the Ballad of Billy and the Howler again.

Billy's Trip

Time went by and more and more people became interested in the Ozark Howler and in Billy Bob. Of course many people still said that it was just a boy with a big imagination but enough people believed the stories to keep them alive. We all know that it's fun to think about things like the Howler, isn't it?

Finally some people in Chicago decided that they would put an end to the nonsense about the Ozark Howler and all of the other creatures that they called "mythical." They invited Billy and his parents to come to Chicago and to answer questions at Northwestern University. They sent train tickets and hotel reservations and even offered to take the family on a tour of the big city.

Billy's parents really didn't want their son to be interrogated by a group of people who might not treat him with respect but they trusted the University and they thought that the trip and the tour would be very educational for Billy. "And we will be there just in case," Billy's dad reminded.

So Mrs. Caldwell got a substitute teacher for the school and Rev. Caldwell got someone to fill his pulpit for that one Sunday and the family prepared for their great adventure. To their surprise, when they reached the railroad depot, they found a large crowd of people there to see them off. They understood this to be their local American hero going off to match his own genius with that of the doubters at the great university. It was David and Goliath all over again.

The conductor tapped on his watch and looked nervous as Mayor

Wellman made a short speech and everyone applauded. Several men yelled, "Give 'em what for, Billy!"

Billy's favorite part of the day was when Mary Jean stepped forward and the last minute and said, "Be careful, Billy. I'll miss you." And then she gave him a big hug. Not just a little polite hug but a real, honest-to-goodness hug like he was a soldier going off to war or something.

As he rode along on the train he was watching out the window as the scenery rolled by but he was thinking about the last words he had heard at the station. "I'll miss you."

The beautiful hills and trees and rivers slipped past as the wheels click-clacked on the rails below. The train stopped several times to pick up passengers in big towns like Rolla and little towns like Arlington but they never stayed long. Then they began to go at a slower pace and stop more often as the train approached St. Louis and all of the small towns around the giant city. Billy never new that there could be so many brick buildings in one place or so many people hurrying here and there. He was happy to be in a railroad car instead of on those crowded streets.

Finally the train stopped and began to back up. Within a couple of minutes, they were in a large open building with dozens of trains lined up in parallel fashion under the one enormous roof. "We'll change trains here," his father explained, "so let's get off. We have plenty of time for a little walk and then we'll have lunch at the Harvey House Restaurant.

With each of the three Caldwells carrying their own small carpet bag they walked into the most beautiful building Billy could ever imagine. He couldn't think of anything to say without sounding silly but he was thinking that nothing in Heaven could be any more magnificent than this railroad station. Then they stepped outside in front of the station and Billy saw a broad avenue with tall brick buildings along either side as far as he could see. Directly across the street was a fountain with strange looking people and animals all shooting water into the air. The water fell like curtains back into the pool below.

Billy realized that his mouth was open and he quickly regained himself. His parents were smiling at him and his wonderment. They had been here before and today they were just enjoying the sights again but through Billy's eyes. Then he turned and looked behind him and his eyes lifted upward. He realized that the station was really a beautiful white castle with red roofs and waving flags. Billy had never seen a building more than two stories tall and those were in no way fancy. He was filled with awe.

Lunch at the Harvey House was certainly different than lunch at the Two Sisters Café! It was a huge place and the tables were all covered with white linen. The napkins were also white linen and the silver gleamed. The waitresses were all young and beautiful and they all wore black dresses with white pinafores and white bonnets. Everyone talked softly and smiled at each other. It was very pleasant but Billy did sort of miss the loud and friendly conversations in the Two Sisters. His mother, on the other hand, loved every second of the experience in the Harvey House.

Finally it was time to leave the beautiful restaurant and start back to find the train for Chicago. As they walked between the stores and shops in the station, they noticed that the merchants were all busy hiding things like beer and chewing gum from public view. Rev. Caldwell asked why and one man said that the "saloon smasher," Carrie Nation was getting off of the Kansas City train and they were trying to avoid trouble with her and her followers. Billy's father looked at Billy and said, "I'll explain when we get on the train. There'll be plenty of time to talk then.

In a short time the train left the beautiful station and crossed the biggest river in North America and the tracks turned northward toward Chicago.

****

Billy was amazed at how different two states could be. Illinois was as flat as a pancake and covered with rich black soil. But there were few trees and no hills at all to be seen from Billy's window. Having grown up surrounded by tree-covered mountains, this flat land made Billy feel a little uneasy. "This is too strange," he thought.

The long, straight, flat, rows of green corn made a hypnotic moving pattern as the train cut its way between miles and miles of farmland. Then they were in Springfield and Billy could see the ornate Capitol Building. After another long stop in Bloomington and one in Champaign and several very short stops, they were drawing near Chicago. Billy's father commented, "Isn't it amazing that we can get on the train deep in the Ozarks one morning and be in Chicago that very same day!"

When the Caldwell family stepped off the train they were greeted by two college students holding a sign that said, "Caldwell." When the family approached, the students introduced themselves, took Mrs. Caldwell's suitcase for her and escorted the family to a nice hotel in Evanston and near the University. The next morning, as the family finished breakfast, two more students introduced themselves and said that they would be the escorts to the auditorium where the hearings were being held.

The auditorium was somewhat plain with wooden folding seats

and the walls and ceiling painted white. The walls however were covered with beautiful walnut paneling. The family was shown to some seats on the front row facing a long table in the very front of the room. "When it's your turn," they told Billy, "you will just step up and sit at the table while the professors ask you some questions. Your family will be right behind you."

Soon the auditorium began to fill up with young men and women who Billy guessed were students. They each had a pad and a pencil. There were other, older people there with pads and pencils also. These turned out to be newspaper reporters. Finally a group of even older men came in, sat behind the long table, and appeared not to even notice that all those other people were in the room. They just talked among themselves.

Finally, the man seated at the very center of the long table introduced himself as the Dean of the College of Science and Agriculture then he introduced the other men who were also professors. Some were from the sciences and some were veterinarians.

Before anyone could even catch their breaths, the Dean said, "Young Mr. Caldwell, I believe you are to be our first guest," and motioned for Billy to sit at the table in front of his parents. Even though they were right there, he felt very much alone.

When Billy was seated the Dean asked, "Would you like any water, young man or is there anything we can get for you?"

Billy thanked the Dean and said that he was fine. "I hope you had a pleasant trip," the Dean continued, "and that you will have a chance to visit in our fine city."

It was obvious that the man was just trying to make Billy comfortable. Billy knew that and appreciated it. "You know," the Dean said, "we're all just a little bit jealous of you. We have each had some honors and awards in our lives but no one here has ever had a ballad written about them."

Everyone in the room laughed and Billy smiled. He actually was feeling a little better about all of this. "Billy," the Dean said, "let's just start with you telling us about your encounter with the Ozark Howler. Let's go all the way back to where you were and what you were doing at the time."

Billy had told the story many times so he just recited it again and everyone seemed very interested. Then one of the veterinarians asked some questions about the shape of the animal and what the features of his face were like. He wanted to know about the texture of the fur and the size of the feet.

Another man wanted a careful description of the sounds that the creature made. "Think especially about the time before you threw the fish to him. Did he make any sounds at that time?"

Each of the professors asked Billy several questions and he was usually able to answer them. Sometimes he would just have to say, "I don't know," or "I don't remember."

Finally it was Professor Norrat's turn to ask questions. He looked at the other men and then glared at Billy. "Have you any idea, Child, how much valuable time you're wasting here today. These are important people with important things to accomplish and you tell us fairy tales. What is your childish agenda? What do you hope to accomplish with this charade? Are you hoping to launch another song? Who put you up to this devilish prank?"

"I don't know what some of those questions even mean," Billy replied. "I can tell you what I saw and I can try to describe what I heard but that's really all I can do. And I didn't ask to come here and do this. You asked me to come."

With that, everyone in the room applauded Billy's answer. But the applause just made Professor Norrat even more angry. He looked at the other professors and said, "Has anyone here ever seen one of these things? Of course not! Do you even know anyone who has seen such a thing? Of course not! It's not real and we need to dismiss the whole notion of Ozark Howlers, and Boogey Men, and the Wicked Witch of the West. What nonsense!"

Billy's father was just about to jump to his defense but his mother thought Billy was doing pretty well on his own so she took her husband's arm and kept him in his seat.

Billy calmly said, "Mr. Professor, sir, I'll bet you haven't seen God, and you've never seen the Czar in Russia, or those piranha fish in South America, so does that mean they don't exist?"

The room erupted in wild applause as Professor Norrat's face turned bright red with rage. Mrs. Caldwell noticed that the other professors were chuckling to themselves.

"How much time are we going to waste on this stupid hillbilly boy?" Professor Norrat roared."

That's when Rev. Caldwell finally rose and said, "Gentlemen in our part of the world the term 'hillbilly' is worn as a badge of honor but I doubt if the professor was using it that way. My son was invited here and has shown good manners and great respect toward all of you. In return he has been treated with derision, name calling, and bullying by someone old enough to know better." Then he looked directly at Professor Norrat. "You, sir, are an embarrassment to scientists, to your university, to your city, and to educators in general. Shame on you!"

The Dean who opened the meeting said in a calm voice, "Thank you Reverend Caldwell. Your point was well-spoken and it is well-taken. We apologize to you and to your fine family." Then he looked at Billy. "Son, it's been a pleasure to meet you and you can look forward to receiving a full written apology from Professor Norrat and the rest of us in the very near future." Then he quietly looked at Professor Norrat until the Professor nodded his head in agreement.

The Dean concluded, "I want to thank you all for attending. This hearing is adjourned."

The room erupted in more applause and Billy looked around to see that he was getting a standing ovation. The student who escorted them back to the hotel said, "I still don't know what to think about your Howler but I love the way you put old Norrat in his place. That took more courage than I have and you did it just right. Your good manners gave you the credibility that he threw away because of his bad manners. I'm truly impressed!"

The family stayed for two more days to tour Chicago. They went to the Italian section and Billy got to try a kind of pie made with meat and cheese and tomato sauce instead of fruit. He loved it. They also went to Chinatown where Billy and his parents went to a restaurant called the King Wah and each ordered something different and then they shared so they were able to try lots of different things. On the last day they walked along the shore of Lake Michigan and that turned out to be Billy's most favorite memory of the trip. He had never imagined that a lake could be so big that you couldn't see the other side!

By the time they boarded the train for the trip back home, Billy was eager to go and feeling a little homesick but he was full of wonderful memories of the greatest adventure of his young life.

Bones

As they rode home on the train, Billy was deep in thought remembering all of the events of the trip. He thanked his parents for standing up for him with the nasty professor. His mother explained that she still didn't believe his stories but she wasn't going to let some big city blowhard bully her son. Then she pointed out that it was really Billy's father who stood and put the professor in his place. She smiled at her husband and said, "I was really proud of you when you did that."

While the family was touring in Chicago something was happening that they had never imagined. The auditorium held many reporters who were covering the story and they posted accounts of what had happened in all the area newspapers. But Mr. Bradley, the editor of the Flanders Weekly News, had arranged for one of the reporters to get a report forwarded to him also. This report became a special edition of the Flanders paper and the Caldwell family was depicted as representing the people back at home and making them look virtuous and good.

The story title was "David Meets Goliath in Chicago." The subtitle said, "Just as the boy David slew the enemy Goliath, Billy Caldwell destroyed the hostile professor." It continued, "Instead of a stone in a sling, the boy from Flanders used good manners and logic to win the day."

Billy Bob's train arrived to a large waiting crowd with a brass band and everyone in town cheering. Some held signs that said things like, "Our Hero," or "Flanders's Giant-Slayer," or "Proud of the Caldwells." He saw Mary Jean holding a sign that said "My Hero." The mayor welcomed the family back to their home town and then, with the band playing, they were escorted to their car for the drive into the quiet peaceful woods and their little home. They slept really well for the first time in several days.

****

Where the Current River ripples and splashes between the hills it sometimes cuts down through the limestone creating bluffs and, in the bluffs, it makes many caves. Since the beginning of time these caves have been the refuge of animals and men and today they are places of wonder for young boys and treasure hunters.

Deer and other animals love to graze in the flatland below the bluffs and find protection among the sycamore trees and berry bushes along the banks of the river. Predator animals and hunters find these "bottom lands" below the bluffs to be the perfect place to hunt when the animals graze or go for water. Sometimes the hunters would take their animals into the mouth of the caves and out of the weather. There they could have a small fire and roast the meat in comfort and safety. They often left behind interesting bones and arrowheads, spear points, scrapers, and other tools.

A group of young boys from the Morgan school were exploring one of the caves on a Saturday morning when they came across something they didn't understand. "Look at this bone," one boy said. "It looks like a bone from somebody's arm but it's way too big."

'It must be from a giant!" another boy surmised. One of the fun things about being a human is the opportunity to let your imagination go a little wild. Soon the boys were convinced that a race of giant Indians must have inhabited the cave at some time in the distant past. Thinking that they would be recognized as famous explorers, they took their discovery into town to show it to the newspaper editor and the sheriff.

The sheriff said that he had some business in Rolla so he would take the bone to the college there and ask one of the scientists what he thought. "If you don't mind," the editor put in, "I'd like to ride along." So the next train going north carried the county sheriff, the newspaper editor, and the big strange bone.

When they arrived, they walked over to the college and inquired about who might be the best person to examine the artifact. They were referred to Dr. Anderson who showed great interest in the bone. "This is fairly fresh," he said. "This animal just died recently… definitely a feline structure… it's a femur… I would say with a good deal of certainty that this is from the leg of a cougar."

"Is that like a panther?" the sheriff asked.

"Some folks call them panthers," Dr. Anderson replied. "Panther, cougar, puma, mountain lion – those are all names for the same animal."

"Since it's a big cat," the editor wanted to know, "is it possible that it's from an Ozark Howler? It was found right where the Caldwell boy says he saw a Howler."

Dr. Anderson laughed and said, "I've never seen the bones of a Howler so I wouldn't recognize one if I saw it. I'm just saying that this is from a large cat and the largest cat I know is a mountain lion."

The editor pressed the scientist again, "So you're not saying that this isn't the remains of a Howler."

"I have no way of saying whether it is or isn't a Howler," the scientist stated. "How could anyone know? I'm just telling you that it's from a very large cat and I think it's a mountain lion."

The bone was taken back to Flanders where the boys donated it and it sits there today in the office of the Flanders Weekly News. A note in the case with the bone explains where it was found and gives the names of the boys who made the discovery. It also says, "Possible leg bone of an Ozark Howler."

The Current

Now everything I've told you so far is what Billy or someone else has told me. Remember I didn't live here until a few months ago. But what happened next I saw and experienced. And it made me feel sorry for my friend, Billy, in so many ways.

It was in the spring of the year and the Ozarks are especially beautiful at that time. The air has a fresh earthy smell and a warmth that makes you happy to be alive. The biggest trees have light green leaves popping out all over and the smaller trees like redbud and dogwood are blooming in beautiful pinks and whites. The ladies' lawns are full of bright yellow daffodils and a person just has to realize how much they have missed the colors of warm weather.

The rivers and streams are rushing and full in the spring making their beautiful splashing noises and the fish are hungry and eager for your bait. After enough warm days and nights many people took down their woodstoves and those who didn't, cleaned them out and put pots of flowers on them. Stoves would be of no use for the next few months.

While Billy and I were in school, (of course his mother was there too – she was the teacher.) his father was at home working around the house and thinking about what his sermon should be for the next Sunday. It was such a beautiful day that he started to sing. He was glad to be there by himself because he had to admit that he was a pretty poor singer. Then he got a good idea. "Listening for the Music of God's Creation," he said to himself. Everyone can certainly identify with that.

He had the hoe at the garden spot breaking up the clumps of dirt so the soil would be ready for planting the family's vegetables. Just then Brother Jackson came over the hill and called to Rev. Caldwell. "I've done something pretty bad, Pastor," he said. "I cleaned things up and I can do more but I wanted to let you know first. I went in to clean out the woodstove but I started a fire in it first. My idea was to smoke out any chimney sweeps or other birds that might be wanting to nest in there. Then I could seal off the chimney."

"Well sir, I went back down and let the fire burn out and shoveled the coals and all of the old ashes into a big steel bucket and set them by the stove while I finished working with the chimney. I locked up and started for home when I had finished. I was almost home when I commenced to worrying about those coals and ashes. I just didn't remember taking them outside.

"Sure as shootin, when I got back in sight of the church, there was smoke commin' out from under the doors and I knew I'd created a whole passel of trouble. I ran back in and got the bucket and threw it out the front door. I looked around for flames but couldn't see any but the smoke was so bad that I had to get out to breathe. When I could, I went back in and found that the floor was still a-smokin' where the bucket had been. I got some water from the well and threw it on there.

"Now that put out the fire, Reverend, but it surely is an ugly place on the floor. I want to assure you that I'll sand it and varnish it and whatever else needs to be done. It'll look new again soon – even if I have to replace that part of the floor. But here's the bad news. All of the Bibles and other books in there 'stink to High Heaven' as they say. I opened them up and laid 'em on the pew benches to air out and I also left the doors and windows open while I came here. I'm on my way back now to work on the mess but I just wanted you to know that I did it and that I'll be eternally sorry."

Rev. Caldwell got a serious look on his face and looked toward the distant tree tops while Mr. Jackson waited in fear of what he might say. Finally the minister said, "If you put those stinky books in the benches, it gives a whole new meaning to the word, 'pew' doesn't it?" Then he broke into a big smile.

"You're a good man, Pastor!" the relieved Mr. Jackson roared as he laughed at the joke and in his great relief. "I'll go now and get back to work. Thank you, Reverend."

"I'll be along in a few minutes," Rev. Caldwell answered. I have some notes to write about my sermon and a couple of things to check on. Then I'll be along."

Mr. Jackson left and he was the last person to see Billy's dad.

****

The things that Mr. Caldwell wanted to check on were his little Brown Swiss heifer and her new calf. He hadn't seen them and once he thought he heard the heifer bawl. They had been at the edge of the forest that morning so he went in that direction. He was walking into the woods when he realized that he still had the hoe in his hand so he leaned it up against a tree so he could find it when he came back.

He continued on for a few minutes and then thought he heard something. "I hope it's not the Howler," he said to himself and smiled. Then he thought, "Two jokes in ten minutes. That's pretty good for me!" It was true – he wasn't much of a jokester.

The next time he heard the sound he recognized it as Sally, his Swiss cow. She was bawling for help and he soon realized why. When he found her she was standing at a washed out part of the riverbank and her calf had fallen onto a muddy shelf below. The Current River was moving fast and busily eating away at the little dirt shelf where the calf stood crying for its mother.

"Just look what your child has gotten into!" he said to Sally. "I sure wish I had a rope with me. If I go home and get one, I'm afraid the rest of the dirt there will be carried away and your calf with it."

Sally stood and looked intently but kept on bawling. "All right, all right," Mr. Caldwell declared. "You're not helping anything, Sally. Just be quiet and let me do my job!"

He held a tree root that protruded from the riverbank and climbed down onto what little remained of the dirt "shelf" where the baby stood. Putting his arms under her belly, he lifted her into the air but his weight and hers made him sink into the mud so deeply that he could hardly pull his feet free. When a big section of the "shelf" broke away and fell into the raging water, it freed his right foot and he took a step onto a muddy spot that was more solid for the time being. With his right foot in place, he was able to pull his left foot free and step forward enough to set the calf up onto the grassy bank with her mother.

She licked the calf all over and walked toward home with the baby trotting behind. Then Rev. Caldwell saw her stop while the baby had a long-overdue meal. "You're welcome," he called out to the pair. Then to himself he said, "Not so much as a thank you!" and reached for the tree root to pull himself back to safety.

But, just at that moment, the entire shelf of dirt washed away and he fell headfirst and backward into the raging cold waters of the Current River. In August or any time in the winter months he would have been able to stand up in the water at this spot. But now the river was running wild with the spring runoff. Both the depth and the current worked against him.

Mr. Caldwell managed to get his head above the surface and gasp for air but he was being carried quickly downstream. In the distance he saw a tree that had fallen into the water from the west bank. He tried to swim through the current and toward the west bank. After a terrible struggle he was able to reach for a protruding branch of the fallen tree. It was wet and slimy but he managed to catch a hold. Then his hand slipped and the current threw him forward again.

This time his right leg caught in a fork of some large branches which were submerged under the water. He felt his right leg snap and break there in the fork of the tree and the strong current pulled him under to the level of his snagged leg. He managed to raise his head one last time and gasp for air and then went under again. With great effort and terrible pain, he reached with both hands and pulled his leg from its trap.

He was free again and he could breathe again but he was still at the mercy of the rushing water. Being a religious man, he thanked God for helping him to get free and asked to be spared from this watery death. "Billy still needs me," he reminded God.

Another fallen tree, this one completely free, came floating by and Rev. Caldwell managed to get a hold on one of its branches near the trunk. He held on for his life but every time the tree bumped into something on the river's edge or bottom, it would jerk violently and try to throw him off. It managed to do that twice but he managed to grab another hold on his uncooperative lifeboat.

At some point he realized that he was floating downstream toward the Black River and Arkansas. There was a tiny village downstream called Mason's Mill but he didn't know about that. He just knew that he was floating deeper and deeper into the wilderness of the Ozark Mountains.

****

Knowing that he couldn't let himself drift any deeper into the wilderness, and knowing that he wouldn't be able to keep his grip on the moving tree that often tried to throw him off, he decided to look for an opportunity to get to the riverbank. At one point the top of the great tree hit the east bank and went into a swirling motion carrying the trunk toward the west bank. As it did this, Mr. Caldwell ducked under the fast-moving trunk and let it move over him. When he came up he swam to the best of his ability toward the west bank. His painful broken leg was of no help and it hindered him greatly.

With great effort he managed to reach the west bank of the river and grab onto a tiny tree root that was protruding into the water just below the surface. He pulled himself toward the bank and realized that he was worse off than before. The riverbank here was about eight feet high and made of red clay mud. There wasn't anything on earth more slippery than that. There was absolutely no way to climb out of the water at this place.

The man clung to the tree root there in the freezing cold water and breathed deeply trying to think of a way that he could escape. His body ached and his mind was tired. He was trying to think but his brain was filled with fog. Finally he began to slide on his stomach holding on to anything his hands could find and work his way downstream looking for any opportunity to climb out.

Then he saw it. It wasn't a stairway or even a boardwalk but it looked almost as good. Another fallen oak tree lay there but this one was still mostly on the riverbank and several of its large branches were dangling into the river. Like climbing a ladder with his hands and one foot, he pulled himself up onto the grassy riverbank, gave thanks to God and fell into a deep sleep.

Castaway

Rev. Caldwell awoke in the dark of the night shivering violently in his wet clothing. "I may be miserable but I'm alive," he thought. Then he added the thought, "Alive for how long?" He decided to keep his clothing on even though it was wet. Then he reached out and gathered all of the dry leaves he could find and pulled them closer. He squeezed as close and as far under the log as he could. Finally he pulled the leaves over himself for insulation and decided to take his chances.

"In the morning I'll try to build a fire," he told himself. "There's a lot of material here to burn but I don't know how I'll start a flame." Soon he was back to sleep and the leaves did a pretty good job of keeping the cold night air away.

When he finally awoke, he realized that the sun must have been up for quite a while. The good news is that the violent shivering had stopped but when he removed his blanket of leaves he still felt very cold. "I'll have to tough it out," he thought. "I need to sit in the sun and get these clothes dry or I'll never be warm."

He pulled himself out into the sunlight and, with both hands, moved his broken leg around where he could examine it. It was every bit as bad as he thought but now he saw that there was also a cut near where the break had happened. There must have been blood vessels broken under the skin because the leg was swollen and blue. The blood on his skin had already clotted. "It's twelve or fourteen hours since the injury, "he thought. "That's a long time to go without cleaning a wound. I hope it didn't get infected." He sat there in the warm sun for a time letting his clothing get dry and trying to think.

"I read that story," he thought, "about Robinson Crusoe and felt sorry for the guy! But he had a whole ship full of supplies just a short distance away from his nice warm beach. He didn't have any broken bones either. In fact he had a friend and helper there for whatever he needed or wanted. That guy had it made! But I'm a castaway here in the deep forest and I have none of those things."

He shifted his weight a little and got himself set for some serious thinking. "OK," he said to himself, "here's the way things stand:

1. I'm in a place where no one lives. So there is no one to help me.
2. The river only travels one way. If I wanted to ride it somewhere, it would take a long time to get to somewhere where a town might be – probably somewhere in the next state.
3. I have plenty of water but no food.
4. My leg is broken and I don't know how to set it.
5. If I make a crutch, I might be able to walk for a short distance but I'll never make it back to the house."

Then he thought of what he might do to help himself.

"1. I could write some messages on pieces of wood and throw them into the river. Of course I don't have anything to use for writing.
2. I could start a fire and make smoke to signal people who might be looking for me but I don't know of any way to start a fire out here . . ."

That's when he realized – "There won't be anyone looking for me way out here. No one knows that I was at the riverbank. No one will be looking for me way out here!"

The News Arrives

I'll never forget that day at school. It was the middle of the afternoon and we were reciting our lessons while the younger kids were practicing their reading and arithmetic. A man I don't know came into the school and went straight up to Mrs. Caldwell. I remember that she turned pale and he eyes got wet and then she said, "Children, we'll be dismissing early today. Be sure and finish your lessons at home. You are dismissed."

She gave Billy Bob a funny look and waited until the other children were gone. I waited just outside the door and heard her tell Billy the news. "Billy," she said. "Something has happened and your father is missing. He was expected at the church this morning but he didn't arrive. Several men have been looking all along the path and along the road but have found no trace of him. The automobile is still under the tree at home."

"Let's go, Mother," Billy said, "I want to help them look."

I'll have to admit that I thought about the Ozark Howler when I heard the news and I found out later that lots of people were thinking the same thing. When Billy and Mrs. Caldwell came out of the school he saw me standing there but didn't say anything. I wanted to help more than anything but I didn't know what to do.

As soon as I got home I told my mother what had happened and that I wanted to go and help. She understood completely but made me eat a sandwich and drink some milk before I left. Soon I was with a group of men walking along both sides of the path between the house and the church calling out for Rev. Caldwell at the top of our lungs and then getting quiet and listening for any kind of reply. Of course no reply was ever heard. We couldn't have known that he was many miles away under a log in the wilderness.

Billy Finds a Clue

I felt like I had wasted the whole afternoon and evening searching the area that had already been searched at least a dozen times before but the men weren't going to send me out into the wild country so I could get lost too. So I decided to go to Billy's house and help with the chores or do anything else that I could.

When I arrived I saw that the Sheriff and a deputy were there already. They were asking Billy and Mrs. Caldwell about any ideas they might have as to where to look. "We just can't find any trace of him and don't know where to look for a trace," the Sheriff said.

Billy saw me and asked if he could be excused. The Sheriff said he could but added, "You be sure and tell me if you think of anything."

Billy promised he would and later wished he had kept his promise but the fact is that he didn't. We left the house and I helped him to gather the eggs, put some hay out for Sally even though she seemed content with the new onion-filled grass that was all around. Some of the stuff we did was just because neither of us could stand to be still.

He suggested that we might want to break up some of the dirt clods in the garden but we couldn't find a hoe anywhere. "That's really strange," Billy said because my dad just cleaned and oiled the hoe. Then he hung it right here."

Billy took off walking really fast toward the garden and I stayed right on his heels. "Look at this!" Billy said. "My dad was working in the garden today! And where did he put the hoe?" We looked all around for it and all at once Billy shouted. "It's over here in the woods. It's leaning up against a tree nice and neat. Dad was working in the garden and then came over here!"

His mind must have been going a million miles and hour and I couldn't keep up with him. We ran up to his house to tell the Sheriff but the Sheriff was already gone. Billy excitedly told his mother what he thought but she wasn't as enthusiastic about the idea as Billy.

"A hoe leaning against a tree might not mean that much," she told Billy but it's worth checking out. "Run now and tell the men what you've found."

"Where are the men now?" Billy asked. "Mom, if Dad's in trouble in the woods, he might need help right now. What if he's hurt? We'll go look for him. You go and tell the men that we're looking in the woods."

Reluctantly she agreed and left for the church where the search had been centered. Billy and I ran to the woods and wandered finding no trace of anyone until we eventually came to the river. "Look over here," Billy said. "There are hoof prints all over the place. Lots of big ones and some little ones too. That would be Sally and the calf. There must have been some trouble here and Dad came to help."

"Oh, Billy," I said. "You don't suppose he fell into the river?"

We walked down steam for a long way yelling and calling for an answer but none came. There were no footprints and no sign that any human had ever been there since the beginning of time. Billy became very serious and very quiet. "If he fell into the water," he said flatly, "he may have been washed off for some distance. If we take a boat, we can look for him as we float." Then he added, "I'm doin' it. Are you with me?"

"If we go, we may have a frightful walk back," I said. "We'd better be prepared. Do you even have a boat?"

"Yes and no," Billy replied. "You're right about being prepared and no, we don't have a boat. So I'm going to get some stuff together for us and you run over to Tribble's and ask to borrow their rowboat. I'll be ready by the river when you get there."

****

I ran as fast as possible through the forest undergrowth to the Tribble's place. But there was no one at home. I knew that I might be getting in trouble but I couldn't let Billy down so I took the boat anyway. "This is his father," I told myself. "If I let him down he would never forgive me." I remembered to put two oars and a paddle into the boat and then shoved it into the water.

Sure enough, when I arrived at the riverbank nearest Billy's house, he was there. Sitting with a small pile of supplies, he waved and then helped me to get secured at the shore. We threw the supplies into the boat, scrambled in, and shoved off. I have to admit that I was thinking of helping – that's true – but I was also thinking of having an adventure in a boat and in the great wilderness. It never occurred to me that anyone might be hurt or that the situation might be too big for us.

Doubt

We floated along for a long time seeing no sign of a human presence anywhere but we weren't yet discouraged. As the sun sank behind the western horizon we both knew that we couldn't go on. We found an outcropping of limestone just above the water level and decided to camp there. It was fairly warm but we wanted a campfire so we built one with what nature gave us and with some of the matches that Billy had packed. Soon a cheery little fire was blazing and we were eating sliced ham on biscuits.

As we ate we talked about what to do in the morning. I reminded Billy that it was a long way back and that there was no way to take the boat upstream against that current. "We'll have to walk every step of the way," I said, "and carry the boat through the woods. It'll be a terrible job."

"Yea," Billy answered, "but my dad will be able to help us. The main thing is to just find him. I only hope that we didn't pass him up as he was walking home through the woods and we were floating down the river. He might get home a few days before we do."

"A few days?!" I said. "Billy, we only have enough food for tomorrow! We can't be out here a few days!" He didn't say anything.

Then something else occurred to me. "Billy," I asked, "did you tell your mom that we were going down here?"

Billy looked away toward the far side of the river and said quietly, "She wasn't at home when we left so I couldn't tell her. I intended to leave a note but I was hurrying around so much that I forgot to do it."

"Oh my gosh!" I said. "You mom thinks her husband has

disappeared and now her son too? Oh, Billy, we have to go back right now. She's gonna be worried sick."

"Yea, well, did you tell your mom that we were going?" he demanded. "Your folks think you disappeared too. You're no better than me!"

I realized that he was exactly right. Now everyone would be out looking for the three of us and probably thinking that the Ozark Howler was doing his worst. "Billy, we've gotta start back right now," I said.

"Not yet," Billy stately calmly. "I'm going on for a ways. Then, if I haven't found him by tomorrow night I can turn around and walk home." Then he pleaded with me, "Please go with me for just one more day. I can't carry the boat by myself and you can't either. And I need you here to help keep my head straight. Please?"

****

Even as tired as we were, we didn't sleep very well that night. We were both too worried about the mess we'd made of things back at home. We were mostly worried about our mothers and what they must be feeling. Even though it was spring and the nights were warmer than they had been, we were still fairly cold. Luckily, Billy had brought two old blankets and they helped us a lot. During the night we both must have scooted closer to the fire without realizing it but, by morning, we were shivering a lot. We couldn't have known that just a couple of miles downstream, Billy's father was lying under a log, shivering violently in wet clothes and trying to hold on to life.

After thinking it over all night, I told Billy that morning that I would go on with him for a while but that, even if he went on the next day, I was walking home to tell everybody what was happening and that Billy and I were both safe. He understood and said, "That's a pretty good plan but you forgot one thing. I'll be walking home with you tomorrow and so will my dad. I just feel certain that we're gonna find him today."

We had a couple more biscuits and a few more slices of ham but we decided not to eat them just in case Billy's dad might be hungrier than we were. We also thought that we might need them for the trip home. After that we didn't talk much but just got to work. We carefully doused the fire and made sure we had everything in the boat. We spread the blankets out in the sun to dry because they were damp with the morning's dew. We set the boat back into the water and then stepped from the limestone down into the boat and pushed off.

Billy was as quiet as me and I think he must have been praying too. We were beginning to realize just what a big job was ahead of us and we new that we would need more than luck to get home in good condition. We rode the Current in silence with Billy watching the west bank as I watched the east. We floated deeper into the wilderness and the primitive forest was as inspiring in its beauty as it was in its overwhelming, threatening, lonesomeness. I kept telling myself, "We'll be OK if we just follow the river home," but somehow I knew that was way too simple. There was just too much forest out there for anything to be simple.

We floated onward as the sun rose higher in the sky and I was trying to think of how to tell Billy that it was time to give up and go home. I decided to try and convince him that his father was probably at home right now worrying about him. I had to make it logical and appeal to his good sense. It was getting later and later – I had to say something but how do you convince someone to give up on finding their father?

"Hey! You in the boat!" someone yelled.

My eyes swung to the west bank and I heard Billy scream, "DAD!"

There, leaning against a huge log was a strange-looking Reverend Caldwell. Any time that I had ever seen him he was standing tall and, even if he might be dirty from working in the garden, he always looked neat somehow. He was a proud man – proud in the good way. But today he looked pale and weak and disheveled. He looked like the man I saw once who had been thrown out of a tavern after someone gave him a terrible beating.

I tied the boat to a poplar tree as Billy ran to hug his father. In a few seconds Billy and Mr. Caldwell were sharing what they knew and trying to decide what to do next. I went back to the boat and got the last of the food and a canteen for Mr. Caldwell. "Oh, boys," he said, "I can't tell you how good this food looks! Thank you!"

We talked for almost an hour with Billy and his dad doing most of the talking. I got busy and made a fire to warm Rev. Caldwell because I noticed that he was still shivering and kept his arms crossed across his chest as if he was cold. I also brought one of the blankets from the boat and put it over his shoulders. He smiled at me and pulled it tight around him. He was definitely getting sick.

As we talked, certain things became obvious. None of us had any idea about how to set a broken leg. There was absolutely no way for us to walk home. We were deep in the wilderness where no one would ever find us. We were out of food and had no real shelter if a storm should come. The Current River flowed southward and probably joined with the

Black River but no one knew for sure. Either way, if we floated we would probably go into Arkansas which was even less populated than Missouri. There seemed to be no good solution.

I suggested that Mr. Caldwell should keep our supplies and we could lean the boat over the log making a shelter for him while Billy and I walked back to Flanders. "Did you bring a gun?" Mr. Caldwell wanted to know. "If I'm sitting here injured and weak, I'd be a pretty easy meal for a pack of wolves."

Of course we hadn't thought to bring a gun. "Besides," Billy reminded him, "all we have is a .22 and that wouldn't do any good against a wolf."

Mr. Caldwell looked very thoughtful for a minute and then stated, "I'm actually most concerned about the Ozark Howlers." Then he smiled at himself. Another joke! He was getting good at those.

Billy smiled back at his dad and said, "You're a Caldwell. Those Howlers had better be afraid of you!"

As I said earlier we discussed it for about an hour and then our decision became clear. Our only real hope was to put everything into the boat and let the river take us downstream to whomever or whatever might be ahead for us. One way or the other we had to leave this place.

Downstream

Again we carefully put out our fire and loaded everything into the boat. We laid a lot of green saplings in the bottom of the boat and put one of the old blankets on those so Rev. Caldwell could lie there and not get wet if water splashed in. He put an arm over each of our shoulders and we carried him to the boat where he had a terrible time trying to get in and settle on the blanket. Billy put the other blanket over his dad and we were ready to go.

Just then, I saw another sapling – a sturdy forked sapling. I ran over and, with the hatchet, chopped it off. Then I was in the boat and we shoved off. We were on our way but none of us knew where we were going or even if we would be alive when we got there.

Billy's dad was probably the most optimistic person I ever knew. Even though he was in terrible shape, he kept talking about the beauty of the river. He pointed out all of the big springs that fed the river and made the water so clear. He made sure that we noticed the white limestone bluffs above us and the feathered and furry creatures that surrounded us. He kept us busy with trying to figure out some way to get some of the many kinds of fish that swam by the boat. He never stopped trying to cheer us and give us hope.

That afternoon he asked how much food we had and we had to admit that there was only one biscuit and two slices of ham. "Are you as hungry as I am?" he asked.

We hadn't eaten anything since the night before so we were terribly hungry and admitted to it. So Mr. Caldwell took the biscuit and sliced it in two. Then he put the ham slices on to make a sort of sandwich. After he carefully cut it into three equal pieces, he thanked God for providing such good food and gave us each a section. It was really dry but we had plenty of water so we were fine.

We floated onward until late in the day and Billy and I began to earnestly look for a place to camp. Mr. Caldwell suggested, "You know, boys, that this river is going to take us to safety and it doesn't stop at night. What would you say to floating all night and taking turns sleeping here in the boat? One person could be awake to steer and to watch for a light or any sign of habitation."

"We'll get wherever we're going twice as fast that way," I said and Billy nodded in agreement. So it was decided. We would travel day and night until we found safe haven.

****

We didn't see anything that night but we were OK with that and felt good about how many miles we must have covered. The next day we all watched for a cabin or even a fence or a cow or anything else that would tell us people were there. We saw nothing at all. Mr. Caldwell kept telling us about the beauty of the place and how he hoped it would remain unspoiled but, frankly, I was getting a little tired of hearing about it. I knew that I was just tired period. And I was hungry, and lost, and homesick, and worried. I was trying not to be a grouch but it was hard to do.

"Are there any Indians around here?" I asked.

Mr. Caldwell said that there were probably a few Ouazhigi. "Some people pronounce that as Huzzah and others say Osage. They're supposed to be out in the Indian Territory now but some of them didn't go when they were supposed to. They've always been a friendly bunch so nobody minds if they're around. But I wouldn't count on seeing any of them, if that's what you're thinking. For their own survival, they stay out of sight. I suspect there are some Shawnee too – over from Cape Girardeau, you know."

We floated onward hour after hour. The sun was burning our faces so Billy and I pulled our shirts up over our heads and splashed some water on our faces. We took one oar and laid it across the boat with a blanket over that and made some shade for Mr. Caldwell.

As we traveled, one clear stream after another fed into the Current. They were pure and clean and must have come from nearby springs. The size of the river grew but it continued to move at it's rapid pace. We floated onward for one hour after another. Billy and I noticed that his father was talking less and seemed to be getting pale. But that may have been just the fading daylight.

Night came and went and another day broke. This day brought clouds and that was blessed relieve from the burning sun. No one said anything but we were all hoping that the clouds weren't bringing rain. Billy's dad didn't look like he could take another soaking and another day of cold. He looked pale and weak and like he didn't have much life left in him. I decided that I would look extra hard on both banks for help because Mr. Caldwell's eyes were closed almost all of the time and Billy spent a lot of time looking in the direction of his father instead of toward the riverbanks. The day came and went. The night came and went.

The next morning's light revealed just how bad things were. Billy's dad looked like he was covered with chalk. His face and hands were pale and his eyes seemed somehow deep in their sockets. Billy gave him water to drink but it was food that we all needed. Our bellies ached all the way up into our chests and on down into our guts. It was a bad aching that didn't go away. Then it started to rain.

We scrambled to get a blanket over Mr. Caldwell but it was soaked within a minute or two and the water collected in a pool in the middle of the thing and then dripped in a steady stream right onto Mr. Caldwell. Then we used an oar and the paddle to make the blanket slant and hang over the side and that worked better but the boat was still catching the rainwater and Mr. Caldwell was laying in it. We didn't know what to do.

Billy spoke first. "Maybe we should stop and build a fire to try and dry him out. But if we stop, that just means that we aren't making any progress toward finding help. I don't know what to do!"

I wasn't going to tell Billy what to do if it might mean the difference between whether his father lived or died so I just sat there. Finally Billy said, "I think his best chance is to get him into a house with some food and warmth. And someone who knows how to fix his leg. We have to keep going!"

I just can't imagine how hard it must have been for Billy to make that choice. It seems like it would have been easier to get up on the shore and use the upside-down boat for a shelter and build a fire. Then his father would be warm and dry and comfortable. But I think Billy was absolutely correct. His father didn't have much time left if we stayed in the wilderness.

We stayed in the middle of the river – in the fastest and surest flow. Downstream!

Mason's Mill

We continued on through the wet miserable day and the rain slowed but the clouds hung at the tops of the bluffs threatening to send us a deluge at any time they decided to do so. But they didn't and the rain slowed a little more and then it quit altogether. The clouds moved away toward the east and the afternoon sun shone down from the west. Billy took off his shirt and placed it gently over his father's face so it wouldn't burn any more and we took down his blanket shelter so the sun could dry his wet clothing.

Then we used the blanket as a sponge and got most of the water out of the bottom of the boat. Of course Mr. Caldwell was laying on a blanket and it was soaked but we couldn't think of any way to make that situation better.

For as long as our clothing was damp, we felt cold but gradually the sun dried us and warmed us and we felt a little better. On the other hand, Billy's dad didn't seem to be doing better at all – probably worse. The river was running fast but it needed to be even faster. Mr. Caldwell was running out of time. I didn't tell Billy but I thought that, by morning light, his dad probably wouldn't be with us any more.

I spent the next hour or so trying to think of some way to tell Billy that he had done a good job of trying to rescue his dad and that no one could have done any better. But anything I came up with sounded pretty stupid as I practiced it in my mind. I really didn't want to see the sun come up in the morning because it was probably going to bring the worst day of my life. And it would be much worse for my best friend.

We floated onward and the river got a little wider and a little less deep. Great trees hung out over the east bank threatening to be the next ones to fall into the flow. I was thinking, "Look at you guys. You just take what life brings your way and never worry about it. You live a life on the land and then, one day, you just plunge in and take a trip on the river. Maybe you have the right idea. Don't worry, just take what life gives you and make the best of it."

I know it was silly but that's what I was thinking when I saw something really strange. Hanging from the branch of one of those trees was a really skinny little vine or a really long and skinny snake, or . . .

"Billy," I said, "look at those trees! Do you see anything?"

"Fishing strings!" he said in a whisper. "Somebody fishes here!"

We rowed toward the trees and found two lines tied to an overhanging branch with corks floating a few feet downstream. We tied the boat to the tree and scrambled up the bank. There was a path! We ran up the path for just a few feet and saw them – wooden buildings! A farm! And beyond that, a small town!

****

Billy ran back to tell his father and I ran toward the town. I met two young boys coming down the path from farm. They were on their way to check the fishing lines. I told them that we had a man in the boat and he needed help fast so they took me back to their parents.

The boys' mother ran into town for help and their father went with me back to the boat. He quickly looked at Billy and his dad and then at the broken leg. He looked at us with a very serious expression but didn't say anything. I could see that now, in addition to the swollen red and blue that we had seen before, there was also a distinct green coloring.

Following the man's directions, we put the two blankets together and put Mr. Caldwell on them. Then together we carried him up the little path and toward the farmhouse. We stopped at the neat little cabin where the door was open. We took him inside and found the boys and their mother taking the bedclothes off and getting ready to put new clean bedclothes on a small bed at the side of the only room.

Even in his terrible condition, Mr. Caldwell was a true gentleman and he said, "Mam, I appreciate your kindness but I'm wet and dirty and will just soil your sheets as soon as I touch them. Please let me lay on something old until I'm strong enough to clean up."

She quickly put a tattered quilt on the bed and doubled it over. We took Mr. Caldwell from his blankets and helped him settle on the bed. He looked around and smiled and fell into a deep sleep.

The lady of the house quickly stirred up the fire in the fireplace and swung a kettle over it. "When was the last time you boys ate?" she asked.

We looked at each other and Billy finally spoke up. "I think it was three days ago, Mam. We shared a biscuit and some ham." Then he quickly added, "But we've had plenty of water to drink so things could have been worse."

She smiled at us and took some bowls from a little shelf. None of them matched but they were all clean and so were the big spoons she brought out. She gave them to us and said, "Come over by the fire, boys. I have some good venison stew in the pot but I'm going to start you boys off with just some watered-down broth from it. If your stomachs handle that OK, then we'll fish out some meat and potatoes for you too. We'll do the same for your father when he's awake again."

Several men and women arrived at the door and stood around the edge of the room. Mr. Caldwell slept for a long time and we told our story as best we could. Finally everyone decided that we should wake him and get some of the good broth into him. He seemed surprised to see all of the concerned faces gathered around and was clearly happy to see and smell the bowl of broth. Before he took his first sip, he thanked God for the food and for the Samaritans who helped them.

Everyone noticed and appreciated his words. Billy and I realized that we hadn't said anything. We just took the food and offered no thanks. We were a little bit ashamed of ourselves.

One well-dressed man who looked like he might be a merchant took a step toward us and said, "Boys, we know about your ordeal but tell us more about yourselves. Who are the three of you?"

Billy spoke up and said, "I'm William Robert Caldwell but everyone calls me Billy Bob. This is my father, Reverend Moses Caldwell, and this is my best friend Roger Blankenship. We all live near Flanders in the Morgan area and my mother is the teacher at the Morgan Schoolhouse."

I told a little about my family and then added, "Is there any way at all that we can get word to them that we are all OK? They must be frightful worried."

One boy just a little older than us offered, "If someone will write down what you want to say, I'll take the message to the Sheriff's office up at Ironton. I think that's the closest telegraph."

Everyone agreed that it was a good plan and it must be done first thing in the morning. One man offered his horse for the boy to use. It must have been a good horse because the boy was very pleased to hear the offer.

The well-dressed man looked at the three of us and said, "You know probably that you can't stay here. Somehow you'll have to get up to Ironton too if you're going to save that leg. There's an old doctor up there who's seen it all. He'll know what's best for you."

While everyone was talking, the lady of the house had been watching Billy and me and she saw that we were doing fine with the broth in our stomachs. She collected our bowls and ladled out some more broth with some chunks of tender meat and some vegetables. The meat was good but had quite a gamey flavor. The potatoes chunks were wonderful and the carrots were even better. This time we remembered to thank her kindly and to silently thank God for providing these fine people and the nourishment they shared with us.

We could see through the door that it was completely dark outside now and the others began to leave. Someone whispered something to the well-dressed man and he turned to us one last time. "We're just dyin' to know – You're from Flanders and your name is Billy Bob – are you the boy in the song?

Billy admitted that he was and everyone smiled, laughed, and left in a raucous fashion. Billy Bob Caldwell became the very first celebrity to ever visit Mason's Mill, Missouri and it still tells that in their history book today.

We realized that we didn't even know who our hosts were so I asked them about themselves. In short, they were the Emerson family and they had a small farm adjoining the spot where the little cabin stood. They had given Mr. Caldwell the bed where their boys usually slept and the boys were gladly spending the night at the home of some friends. Billy and I were assigned a place to sleep on the floor near the fireplace.

Many people in that part of the country were said to be "dirt poor" meaning that they had dirt floors. But the Emersons had a nice clean wooden floor and a snug home with a tight roof. There would be no dew on our blankets tonight. We slept that night feeling secure for the first time in several days.

Ironton

As promised, the boy on the borrowed horse did go to Ironton and the Sheriff there sent the telegraph at his own expense. We didn't know it but, when the news reached Flanders, there was great rejoicing and people gathered around the bandstand where a small celebration was held and everyone sang together, Come Thou, Font of Every Blessing.

The mayor reminded them that they would feel even better one day soon when all three of their friends were back at home and all in one piece. Everyone understood that the last part of that referred to Mr. Caldwell's leg. The telegraph only described it as a "severely injured right leg."

****

Before long Billy and I were back to our normal strength and Mr. Caldwell was even doing a lot better. There was still no way for him to walk even with the crutch I had made. He suggested that two crutches might do a better job for him. I think he was just trying to keep Billy and me busy so we wouldn't worry so much.

We had brought back another strong, forked sapling and were trying to fashion a crutch identical to the first one when Mr. Emerson called us into his home. There he, and Mrs. Emerson, and Billy, and his father, and I all gathered in a circle to talk things over.

Billy's dad spoke first. "I can't think of how we might be able to repay you for your kindness. But I'll promise you this, when we get home I'll do whatever I can to get some extra money together and send you something to make up for the food we've eaten and the time that we've taken you from your fields."

"One thing is certain," he continued, "we'll never be able to get that boat back to its owner. I'll have to buy our neighbor a new one. But you can keep this one. It's a good boat and your boys will soon be catching the biggest fish around. You can also use it to get back and forth across the river. It's the least we can do to thank you."

Mr. Emerson answered, "You would have done the same for us. Don't think another thought about paying us. We have everything we need right here. I do need to talk to all of you about what comes next. You are strong enough now to make the trip and we have to get you to that doctor in Ironton. Your leg is getting worse – not better."

Billy and I didn't know it but that greenish color we had seen was gangrene and it was spreading. It kills a person pretty quickly if they don't deal with it.

Mr. Emerson continued, "We've arranged to use Mr. Benton's buckboard and his team. It's the best in town and you'll be able to lay out flat for the whole way. The Jasper boy who went to Ironton on horseback knows the way and he'll go along to help. It will take two days if all goes well but we've rigged a canvas top on the wagon to keep you safe and dry so you should be fine. Will you be up to leaving in the morning?"

Billy's dad said, "I'll be as ready in the morning as I'll ever be."

We didn't know exactly how true that was. He hadn't said anything discouraging to us but he knew the gangrene was getting worse every day. We went back outside to try and finish the second crutch before dark. All in all, we did a pretty good job and I think he was happy with it.

****

Even before the sun came over the mountains we were in the back of the wagon and the driver and his guide sat up on the bench seat. The horses were four big strong beauties and we knew they could pull our little load with no trouble at all.

We sincerely tried to find something good to say and express how grateful we were to the Emersons and to the rest of the people but nothing we said was nearly good enough. The wagon bounced along from the Emerson cabin and up into the town. It was a surprisingly nice little place, clean and prosperous-looking. Many of the townsfolk walked along with us into town. One man noticed Mr. Caldwell wincing every time the wagon hit a bump. He ran ahead and returned with a bottle of bourbon whiskey "for the pain."

Mr. Caldwell refused saying that he didn't drink but the man explained, "I'm not telling you to get drunk. I'm just saying that you should take it in case that leg gets so sore that you need some medicine. It can't hurt to have it along." Mr. Caldwell nodded his head and thanked the man. Then he put the bottle under the other contents in the wagon.

For almost fourteen hours we bounced along the rough road which was really not a road at all. It was just a place where the trees had been cut to allow wagons to pass. Most of the stumps were still sticking up trying to grab the wagon axles as they passed over. Usually that was not a problem. But, at one place where the wagon wheel ruts had grown deep, the front axle scraped to a stop on top of one of the large stumps.

The driver pulled back on the reigns and yelled "Back! Back!" to the horses. They tried to back up but couldn't. Then "Giddyap" as he tried to go forward again. No luck.

"What's wrong?" I asked from the back of the wagon.

"I'm stumped," the driver answered. "I can't go forward and I can't go back. Nothing I try works."

So we all climbed out of the wagon and chopped off some strong young trees to use as levers. With them, we lifted the front axle over the stump and slowly pulled the wagon forward to see if the rear axle would clear. It wouldn't. So we put our levers and everything else we could find into the ruts and, when the rear wheels rolled up onto those things, the rear axle cleared the stump easily.

The rest of the trip went smoothly but, while we were camped that night, Billy noticed that his father was tossing in his sleep. He put his hand on the dad's forehead and said, "He's got a fever. This can't be good."

It was late the next day when we rolled into Ironton. It was a beautiful place in a wide valley. It had many brick buildings including some old mansions. We rolled past a gigantic dirt circle in the valley that we later found out was the remains of an old Civil War fort that was used to stop General Price from attacking St. Louis.

A man on the wooden sidewalk told us how to find the doctor's office and we were in luck – he was in. Dr. Jorgensen was a very old man but he looked fit and healthy. He helped us to carry Mr. Caldwell into his office where he immediately cut away the right leg of the blood-stained smelly trousers. He looked at the leg and then looked at us. With a cloth and soapy water he cleaned off the swollen leg and looked at us again.

The old doctor stepped outside of his office and motioned for us to step out with him. Once the door was closed he said, "Boys, you probably already know what I have to tell you. Your father's leg has to come off. I just hope we're not too late."

I didn't say anything and neither did Billy for a while. Finally Billy said, "I think we should take him home and let my mother know about this."

"There's no time for that," the doctor insisted. "He has gangrene and it's spreading. If it goes any further, it'll be into his gut and he's lost."

"How much has to come off?" Billy wanted to know.

"At least a few inches above his knee," was the answer.

Billy stood silent for a time and then said, "You have a railroad here. Can we put him on the train and take him to St. Louis? There might be some better doctors there."

I winced when he said that. It was pretty insulting to Dr. Jorgensen but the old doctor didn't bat an eye. He just said, "You have two choices. Either he goes home without that leg or he goes home in a pine box. Look, boys, I was a corpsman in the War Between the States and a doctor in the Spanish-American War. I've seen a lot of gangrene but I've never seen anybody with a worse case than this who survived. Even if we amputate, that doesn't mean he's going to live. But if we don't take the leg, your father will die right here – and before long. Let me know what you decide." With that he turned and went into his office closing the door quietly behind him.

We stood outside and talked for a bit. "He's a gruff old guy," I said, "but he's just being honest with us. He's treating us like men instead of sugar coating things like we were children."

"I know," Billy answered. "I just hate to decide such a terrible thing."

We stood in silence and I watched Billy experience the torment that no eighth grade boy should have to endure. It was easier for me to understand what the doctor was saying and agree with him but I couldn't imagine how Billy could ever make the decision to have his father's leg sawed off. Billy looked at me and right into my eyes. I think he wanted me to tell him what to do but I couldn't. It wasn't my choice.

"Doc Jorgensen thinks we're brothers," I said after a while.

"I think he's right about that," Billy replied. Then he put his hand on my shoulder and turned me around. He guided me into the office where the old doctor sat writing some notes in a thick book.

The doctor didn't say a word. He just looked up at the two of us. "We've decided," Billy said, We've decided to go ahead. Take it off." Then he turned and was out the door again. We sat outside leaning against the building and didn't say anything for a long long time.

A young woman eventually came and entered the building. She didn't look ill and I thought she must be some sort of nurse or assistant for the doctor. Then Dr. Jorgensen came out and found us. "When was the last time that you boys ate anything?" he asked.

"This morning, sir, when we broke camp," I told him. He gave us a note and sent us to the little café about a block away.

"This tells Jenny to give you whatever you're hungry for," he said and then he shooed us away toward the business buildings. Billy said he didn't have an appetite yet but I understood that the doctor was wanting us to be far away in case Mr. Caldwell screamed or anything.

"Well, I'm hungry," I lied to Billy. "Come on and order something and I'll eat yours too."

We found the café and went in. There were a few people in there and they all turned to look at us. I wondered how much they knew or were they just curious about two ragged looking strangers in town? That was the first time that I realized just how ragged and terrible we must look. "Of course we're a mess," I thought, "but I just wasn't mindful of it until now."

We spent a long time in the café and then gave Jenny the note from Dr. Jorgensen and walked back to his office. We didn't even think that maybe we shouldn't go in yet so we just strolled in. To our surprise, the operation was complete. The whole office had a terrible stink about it. There was the smell of medicine but there was a rotten smell too and I knew that must be from the blood and the infected leg.

Rev. Caldwell laid on the table still with a fresh sheet over him. He just looked like he was sleeping but he was extremely pale. I looked at his leg and it wasn't where it should be. It was completely gone. I knew that it would be but it still shocked me to see the sheet laying where his leg should be. I could also see that, under the clean sheet, there was a very bloody sheet that Mr. Caldwell was laying on. Some bloody surgical instruments and a square bloody saw lay on a small table next to the big one. Dr. Jorgensen's assistant said, "We're not quite finished cleaning up, boys. Please wait outside."

We sat outside again without talking and I wondered, "Where is the leg? What do they do with something like that? How do they stop the bleeding? How much of that did Billy's dad feel? Did he scream? Will he remember any of it? Is there anything that I should have done?" I thought of all the war veterans that I have seen and all of the men who lost part of them in farming accidents. They were brave in ways I never realized before. And I knew that I would never be the same after today.

Recovery

As we sat outside the doctor's office the world was going by but we were paying no attention to it. Oh, we knew that there were wagons and horses and several automobiles sputtering in the street. And we knew that men and women and children were there but we didn't really notice any of them. We didn't see the two who came up the boardwalk until they stopped right in front of us. We looked up and realized that it was the two who had brought us up from Mason's Mill.

"How's the Reverend?" they wanted to know. "Is he gonna make it?" We told them everything that we knew and somehow felt a little better after telling it all. It seemed to make a little more sense when we put it into words.

They listened to every word and explained that the people in Mason's Mill would want a full account of what transpired. Finally the man who had been driving said, "You're a tough couple of fellers, you are!" and they left.

****

Eventually Dr. Jorgensen invited us back inside. "Boys," he said, "you will have to care for him for a while. I'll show you what you need to do for him." He still thought we were brothers so I stood there and saw things that I really didn't want to see. I stood there for Billy. The doctor removed the sheet and revealed the large muscles and the tied blood vessels and the stump of bone with saw marks across it. It looked like something we would see when cattle or hogs were butchered but this time it was a person. It was Billy's dad!

Billy paid close attention through his tear-filled eyes and when I saw him crying, I couldn't help it, I cried too. But we listened and we learned. It would be up to us.

After a time the gruff old doctor put his arms on our shoulders and walked us out of the office. He gave us each a hug and said, "You're doing fine, boys. Just fine. Now the Reverend is going to sleep for quite a while and you need to give him the time he needs. I'll call you when he starts to wake up."

Never getting too far from the doctor's office, we wandered around the pretty little town and tried to think about other things. We talked about how we would get home and when. We figured that we would probably have to take the train but wondered how we could get the money for train fare. While trying to think of jobs we might do, we noticed the railroad depot was close by. "Let's go over and find out how much three tickets would cost from here to Flanders," Billy suggested and we crossed the wide street and the tracks.

As we approached the depot we heard a shrill whistle and saw that the train from St. Louis was just steaming in. We knew the station master would be busy for a few minutes and sat down on a bench there on the railroad platform. People from the city were unloading and being greeted by local people. We asked one lady why so many people from St. Louis were coming to town. She explained that they were arriving for vacations. Ironton was a resort for city families and a good place to get away from the smoke and hustle of the city.

We watched the wealthy families climb down from the train and noticed all of the smiles and anticipation that they showed. It really did cheer us up some but it also made us miss our family and friends back in Flanders. All at once Billy stood up and started to run yelling, "Mom! Mom! Mom!"

Sure enough, there was Mrs. Caldwell stepping down from the railroad coach onto the platform. I ran too. I was almost as happy to see her as Billy was. I was almost there when I saw the second lady step from the train. I grabbed my mother and squeezed her. I had never known that I could miss anyone so much!

****

Within minutes we were at the doctor's office and introducing our mothers to Dr. Jorgensen. When I introduced my mother to him, he looked at me and then smiled. That was when he first understood that Billy and I were just best friends. We checked on Billy's dad but he was still asleep. Our mothers hadn't known about the amputation and Billy's mom bawled a lot but that was fine and we understood.

Dr. Jorgensen said that he had a lot to talk to us about and suggested that we get together in his second office where there was more room. He meant the café down the street. My mother said that we could meet him in a short time but first we had some shopping to do. The doctor looked at us from head to toe and said that would be a fine idea. So, by the time we got to the café to meet the doctor, Billy and I looked like a couple of city slickers in new trousers, shirts, and shoes. We even had new socks and underwear but hopefully no one else knew that.

When we met with the doctor he explained a lot and told us all sorts of things that we would need to do to help Billy's dad learn to do things in a different way. He said that he would need a couple of crutches and Billy and I felt good that we had already taken care of that. He told us that there wasn't hardly anything that Rev. Caldwell had done before that he couldn't do now. He might just need to do it in a little different way.

"Will he be able to play the piano?" Billy's mom asked.

"Of course," the doctor answered.

"Oh good," she replied, "Because he never could before."

We all laughed and laughed. The doctor smiled a huge smile and said, "This man is going to be alright. I know that now. A little humor is the best medicine there is. And I see now where this boy gets his toughness. The Reverend is going to be just fine!"

****

The lady who ran the restaurant told us about a nice boarding house and we arranged for two rooms there. We really didn't know how long we might have to stay. We thought that my mother and I might go back home and Billy might go with us while his mother stayed with Mr. Caldwell but we just didn't know.

When we got back to the doctor's office the sun was already down and the street lamps had been turned on. We knocked on the door this time and Dr. Jorgensen let us in. Mr. Caldwell was starting to wake up and was very groggy. "He's been asleep a long time," the doctor said, "but I think it was mostly his body getting the rest he sorely needed. He probably hasn't had a good deep sleep since the infection set in."

Rev. Caldwell started to mumble something and Mrs. Caldwell put her ear close to his mouth. "He's calling for Billy," she said.

"We're here for you," she told him. Our family is together again and we're here for you."

He opened his eyes and looked directly at her face. We could tell that he was trying to focus his eyes but he smiled a very small smile and his whole body seemed to relax. His hand started to move and Mrs. Caldwell took the hand between hers. Billy stepped forward and stood with them. We probably should have left them alone but it was such a happy sight that we didn't want to go away.

About thirty minutes later, Mr. Caldwell was wide awake and the room was full of happy chatter. The doctor went home and just left us there. Mrs. Caldwell promised to lock the door when we left. To my surprise, Billy's dad didn't seem surprised at all about losing his leg. "I knew that at least some of it would have to go when I first saw the green," he said.

Then he said, "Billy, I didn't want you to worry about me but I thought I would be awake to give the doctor permission. I'm terribly sorry that you had to make such an awful choice. But you did the right thing and I'm grateful to have such a strong and wise son."

The next day turned out to be a Saturday. We had lost track of the time and days. Dr. Jorgensen told us that the wound seemed to be healing with no sign of additional infection. He reviewed the process for cleaning and dressing the leg and talked about some of the other things that Mrs. Caldwell would need to know. Then he told us, "If this is going as well as I think, he'll be resting at home in just a few days. You visit all you want today but allow him plenty of time to rest. Tomorrow I'll try to give you an estimate about when he can leave.

We had breakfast on Sunday morning and went by the doctor's office but Mr. Caldwell was resting. So we went to church and planned to have lunch before going back to the office. It turned out that we couldn't wait so we went to see Mr. Caldwell right after church. When we got there, we couldn't believe our eyes. He was up off the table and practicing with his crutches!

"That's enough," the doctor told him. "You'll have plenty of time to get good with these."

"You did a fine job of making the crutches," Billy's dad told us, "but is there any way you could find some padding for up here under my arms?"

Billy's mom said that as soon as the shops opened on Monday morning, they would find some good padding that would look nice too. "Finally! Something I can do to feel useful!" she said.

A few days later Rev. Caldwell was sitting on the back of a little wagon and riding over to the train station with all of us following behind. At the station we got tickets for St. Louis. At St. Louis we would get tickets for Rolla and then down to Flanders. It seemed too good to be true.

Dr. Jorgensen approached from the direction of his office and said that he wanted to wish us the best. Then he stood awkwardly for a few seconds and said, "There's just something I'm dying to know. Billy, are you the boy from the song?" Billy smiled and nodded his head. "Wooooo Doegies!" the old doctor said. "Just imagine that! Now I have a real story to tell my grandkids." Apparently he told the local newspaper too because the story is still there in a crumbling old newspaper at the library.

A baggage handler and a sturdy salesman lifted Mr. Caldwell up and into the railroad coach and, with his crutches, he managed to get down the aisle to an open seat. He let Mrs. Caldwell go in first because it looked like it would be hard to get across to the seat by the window. Soon he was settled and we all found seats nearby.

While we were boarding the coach, the engine was taken to the roundhouse and turned around to face northward. Within a couple of minutes it was hooked onto the coaches again and we were underway. As the crow flies, Ironton isn't that far from Flanders but we couldn't fly and neither could railroads.

Home!

I had ridden on a train before. In fact, that's how my family came to live in Flanders. But this was really different. When riding with my parents, I had to be all dressed up and I had to sit with them and use my company manners. This time we were trying not to be recognized and pestered so Billy and I were sitting in a completely different part of the railroad car. We talked about all sorts of things and especially about what we saw swooshing past the windows as we sped northward through the Ozark hills.

When we got to St. Louis I was amazed at what we saw in Union Station. We had come to Flanders from Joplin so I had never been to St. Louis. Billy took me all around the place and showed me the whispering arch, the Harvey House, and all of the little shops along the Promenade. When we went outside, I could hardly believe my eyes. The fountain across the street took my breath away with its beauty. Then we did something we shouldn't – we crossed Market Street to the fountain. The cool spray drifted across us in a wonderful way and it was like nothing I had ever experienced.

Then Billy said, "Turn around and look at the train station."

Inside, the building was rich dark colors and lots of lights everywhere. But the outside was gleaming white. It looked like a castle with towers, and red roofs, and flags flying everywhere. I thought that it must be the most beautiful building in the entire world.

When we went back to the adults we found them surrounded by men and cameras. "Reporters," Billy observed. "Someone must have told them that we are here."

"Well, they don't know us," I said so let's just stay over here out of sight.'

I noticed that our parents were looking all around as they talked and figured they must be worried about us. When I got my mother's attention I waved a small wave and she smiled back. Then she whispered something to Billy's mother and she looked our way too.

Finally Billy said, "Let's go," and started toward the crowd. I really didn't want to but I realized then just how much Billy Bob really enjoyed being the center of things. He liked everyone asking him questions and being able to "think on his feet." He enjoyed playing the part of a hero.

Within seconds all of the reporters' questions were showering on us. Each one was looking for some tiny bit of information that they didn't already know. They asked about the decision to make the amputation, and about the journey down the swollen Current River. They asked about our personal likes and dislikes and they especially asked Billy about his experience with the Ozarks Howler. They wanted to know how it felt to have a song written about you.

One reporter asked us if we had girlfriends back in Flanders. I just shook my head indicating that I didn't. Billy, on the other hand, smiled a gigantic smile and everyone knew that he did indeed have a "hometown honey." "What's her name?" they demanded to know.

Billy just continued to smile and said, "She knows who she is – and so do I." That's when I realized something else about my friend. He likes to create little mysteries. He likes to keep people guessing. He really enjoys this kind of thing!

It was just about that time that Billy's dad pointed to the huge clock in the promenade and said that it was time to get to our train. Some of the reporters rushed away to file their stories quicker that the others but some of them stayed behind and offered to help Rev. Caldwell to the train. As Rev. Caldwell struggled through the crowds on his crutches one of the reporters asked, "Now that you'll have to do everything differently, are you worried about getting along back at home?"

We all stopped and Billy's dad answered, "I have a wonderful family, great neighbors, and the best of friends. They won't let anything really bad happen to me or my family. We'll do just fine until I learn my lessons and get along like normal. You come to Flanders sometime and meet the people there. You'll soon see just what I mean."

****

The train ride from St. Louis to Rolla was fun because there were so many young men from the college on board. They were members of a team in a new sport called football and they called themselves The Miners. They had won their game against another school and were full of good spirits. They joked and laughed and sang silly songs. I really liked them!

Of course they got off the westbound Frisco at Rolla and so did we. In a short time we boarded the southbound for the ride to Flanders. We looked forward so much to just getting to our quiet homes. But that wasn't meant to be.

The Boarding Platform at Flanders was filled with people to welcome us home. But, as Rev. Caldwell had noticed, they were good people and good friends and they recognized how tired Billy's dad was and how eager we all were to get home. So they just made us feel welcome and then let us go on our ways without too much of an ordeal. The best thing for Mom and me was seeing Dad again. He grabbed us as we stepped down from the train and hugged us like we had been gone for years. I really loved feeling that man's strong arms around us and that feeling was, for me, what finally brought the long adventure to an end. The safety of my family – all together in this little town that I had grown to love.

****

There is one more amazing thing that I need to tell you about. That evening at the Flanders Depot, everyone in town had arrived before the train and Mrs. Winslow had offered her big black cast iron kettle. Some men hauled it over to the platform and when people arrived, they each dropped in pennies and nickels and some even put in a dollar bill. By the time we stepped off the train, that big stew kettle was completely filled with money to help the Caldwell family.

Everyone knew that the family had missed a big part of the planting time for their garden and that Rev. Caldwell would be doing things much slower for a while. They would have to buy many of the things that they would normally make. But now that worry was over. The kettle didn't contain a fortune but it did contain the medicine to take away the family's worries for a while. The mayor said that it also contained the promise of the town that things would be OK for as long as they needed help.

That was the only time that I ever saw Billy's dad cry. Through all of the terrible things that had just happened to him, he was strong and solid. But it was the kindness of others that melted his heart and we all knew that the tears came from joy and relief. He quietly thanked the people and said, "It's so good to have a town like Flanders to come home to!"

Fix-It Men

When Billy and I got back to school the other kids didn't make too much of a deal about our return. We were the oldest kids in the school so the others always kind of looked up to us anyway. They didn't have many questions because they already knew all of the stories. They seemed most happy to have their regular teacher back. My mom said that it must be very hard to be a substitute teacher but that it's kind of hard on the kids too because they like to have one routine way of doing things. My mom's pretty smart about that kind of thing.

Mrs. Caldwell even told Billy and me that she was relieved to get back to teaching because, when she was teaching, she was too busy to worry about her family. I knew right away that she was right about that. Being busy keeps your mind from wandering into the worries.

Billy's father was the one who had most of the problems to deal with and it wasn't just his missing leg. He said he was really sore under his arms where the crutches go. Even with all the padding on the crutches, his underarms were red and a little swollen. He said he just had to toughen up but that might take a while. It looked to me like he had a lot of problems getting up and down gracefully. He just sort of plopped down and then had to find something to hold onto and pull himself back up. "It's all about leverage now," he said.

My parents said that I could spend all day on Saturdays with Billy so we decided on a list of projects to make Rev. Caldwell's life easier. We became the family's "fix-it men." The first problem was easy. To help him get in and out of bed, we just put a ladder back chair next to the bed and he used it for support.

The front door was a little bit more of a problem. It was very hard for him to step down out of the narrow door onto the rock below the door that served as a step. So Billy and I found some small cedar trees and cut them down to make a handrail. We trimmed away all the branches and cut the trunk of one into three sections. After we sanded them smooth, we planted the two thickest sections into the ground and nailed the skinniest section from the top of the tree onto the top ends of the two other sections. Now Mr. Caldwell had a good sturdy handrail.

We were surprised but not terribly disappointed when he discovered that the rail didn't help very much. What he really needed was a handrail on each side so he could sort of swing down onto the rock and then down again onto the ground. So we made a second handrail identical to the first. Everyone had to admit that they were pretty swell and they worked great.

Next we cut another small cedar and trimmed away the branches. We sanded and cut away two small rails from the top and attached them to the side walls of the outhouse. That way the Reverend could get up or down without calling for help. He said those two rails were the best gift anyone could have given him!

While we were working on the outhouse rails some men came by from the church. They wanted to check on the pastor but they also had some questions about making the church accessible to him. They really liked our ideas about making cedar rails. "They look nice and they'll hold up in the weather," one man commented.

They told us that the burned spot in the floor had been replaced and looked as good as new. They also suggested that they take out the platform in the front of the church where the pulpit stood. That way the entire church floor would be flat. But Rev. Caldwell said he didn't like that idea. “That platform is great for the programs that the kids do,” he said. “It’s just like a stage and people in the back of the church can see even the smallest children. I like having it there. Maybe we could put a handrail on one side so I can get up and down. That would be perfect – and easier.”

So it was decided. A double handrail was erected in the front of the church and at the front steps the men built a rail on one side and one down the middle. That looked a little funny so they built another one on the other side. Later many people, especially the older ones, said they really liked the new rails. The small children loved them and spent a good deal of time swinging back and forth under them.

The men hadn’t thought about rails in the outhouse so they looked at ours and decided to do the same thing at church. Before they were finished they had put rails in the women’s outhouse too. When Rev. Caldwell finally got to see the changes, he loved them and said they should have done those things long ago. One of the older men said, “Since your accident, Pastor – well, we kind of see things through different eyes now.”

The man who had started the fire said, “Pastor, there is one more thing. I’ve been hiding this for a surprise. When you’re up there sermonizing, well, that’s a lot of standing. So I made you this tall chair. Now you can rest on it and preach at us for as long as you like. You know we need it!”

Summer

It wasn't officially summer yet but school was out and it seemed like summer to the kids. The weather was wonderfully warm and everything had turned from the pale yellowish-green of spring to the dark greens of summer. The woods and the farmyards were full of little critters following their mothers around and learning their lessons about what they needed to do. I remember thinking that they went to school all summer but they really seemed to like it. They were all feasting, and growing, and playing, and pretending to be grown up critters.

The farm kids were all busy helping their parents to produce our next year's food and food for the livestock. But the planting was done and mostly they were just cultivating now that the weather was so warm. Almost everyone had chickens and maybe rabbits in our yards and they required fresh water, and food, and lots of cleaning. So the kids were busy with that. In town some of the boys were mowing lawns and making some spending money or helping the family.

Of course I had chores to do for my family but my parents allowed me plenty of time to spend with Billy Bob helping his family and doing "guy things." One of the first things we did was to go fishing at the river. The best spot happened to be in the bright (and hot) sun. So we built a lean-to for our fishing comfort. Soon it had walls and became a clubhouse. We began to store our fishing equipment there and also two gigs for the frogs when they got big enough.

We climbed a huge sycamore tree and hung a rope from a sturdy branch. Climbing down, we tied a knot in the bottom and made a place for our feet while we swung in broad arcs across the clearing. With a strip of leather we bought at the stable, we tied a sapling over and made a "thong tree." Younger boys might sit on the tree and pretend to be bouncing on a horse but we just used it to stand on and spring up and down until we jumped and it propelled us through the air.

By the time late June rolled around it was very hot and humid but that was not a problem for people in the rural areas. Many families had summer kitchens and the ladies began to cook the family's meals in these little kitchens which were really just small houses with cook stoves. They were usually located just outside the back door of the family home. By cooking there, the wood stoves didn't heat up the regular house.

Town people began to sleep at nights on their porches and the children enjoyed sleeping on blankets under trees in their lawns. Farm families often just slept on the lawn – all of them – parents, children, and pets. People who were rich enough would have screened-in porches so they could sleep and have very few problems with pests like flies and mosquitoes. Billy Bob and I had an even better situation. We often went to the cool river valley and slept in or near the clubhouse. Of course we cooked fish, frog legs, and other goodies over our little campfire. To me it was like living in Heaven. When I look back at this, it seems strange to me that Billy never seemed to worry about the presence of an Ozarks Howler. If he thought the creature was real, why wasn't he worried?

More and more I learned to love living in Flanders and my favorite part of living there was all of the camping and companionship I had with Billy. There is no doubt that he was the most interesting person and the best friend I ever had. There was only one thing that interfered with our friendship. Or, it would be more accurate to say that one person interfered.

She didn't do it on purpose and I couldn't blame her for liking Billy. But Billy liked Mary Jean in a different way than he liked me. We had fun but, whenever there was a chance to spend time with Mary Jean, he would leave me behind. Sometimes it really hurt me when I was ignored. And I was ignored any time that Mary Jean wanted Billy's attention. And I had to admit that I saw Billy as a friend but she saw Billy as a hero – and he enjoyed that.

The sad thing is that, at our little one-room school, there weren't any girls our age. Mary Jean went to the High School because she was a year older than us. She told me once that for the freshman year of high school, kids from dozens of little schools all across the county would come and meet each other for the first time. "There'll be lots of girls," she told me, "and I know for sure that you'll be very popular next year."

What she said seemed to make sense so, now that I graduated from eighth grade, I began to look forward more and more to next year at Flanders High School. I wanted to learn how to play a musical instrument and be in the band. After seeing St. Louis, I wanted to learn more and more about the big cities in the world. I was anticipating the basketball games and learning about football. Most of all I think I looked forward to meeting all of those girls that Mary Jean had promised.

Howler Days II

As the summer wore on, the question came up about whether or not the Howler Day should be held again. The business people insisted that they made a lot of extra sales that day. The mayor said that, in spite of the skunk invasion, people still went home thinking positive thoughts about Flanders. Soon it was decided that there should be another Howler Day celebration. The next question was about how they might make it better.

"Bigger and better!" the mayor said. He suggested that they might want to start the celebration on Friday evening and continue it through Saturday and Sunday. The other members of the Council said they thought maybe they should develop the festival in steps and not jump too far all at once. In the end they decided to have the Saturday festival just like the previous year and then a community church service on Sunday morning. Finally, there would be food, music and other entertainment until Sunday afternoon.

Committees were formed to advertise, to get musical groups, to let the vendors know to bring their food and booths. The mayor offered to arrange for some very interesting speakers. Of course he meant Billy Bob and the Mayor himself. The local ministers were happy to arrange a community church service. Just like that Howler Day turned into Howler Days.

****

When the big day arrived many things went on much as they had the year before. Just as she did last year, Mary Jean went to a spot near the bandstand and set up her booth. That guaranteed that she would have the best spot as she sold her drawings. This year she also had drawings of Billy Bob and me rowing the boat with poor Rev. Caldwell riding through the wilderness. Other vendors had learned from Mary Jean and they also arrived on Friday evening choosing prime locations for their booths, tents, canopies, and lean-tos. By the time street lamps were turned on Friday night, the town already had the main street lined with booths, banners were flying, and the stores and courthouse were decorated with bunting.

This year the merchants also sponsored an art contest for all of the school kids. Small prizes were awarded in different age groups but, even if they didn't win a prize, each artist got to put their name on their work for everyone to see. The art work was painted onto the plate glass windows of the different stores, the bank, the café, and every other business that was big enough to have a glass display window. The kids were furnished with a kind of paint made from egg yolks called tempera paint. It changed the entire appearance of the main street and everybody loved it!

Early on Saturday morning the vendors and storekeepers arrived and began to display their wares. Fires were lit and great kettles of food began their slow boils to provide fine soups and stews for the visitors. Fish were being cleaned and breaded in anticipation of large crowds of hungry people. The crafters were there again with the brooms, baskets, and handmade utensils. Of course the Madison Stable once again offered a new Ford in a very popular raffle.

The younger kids loved a new booth that was operating this year. The ladies of the Gilead Church had set up a booth to paint the faces of the children. Some of the little boys wanted their faces painted red to look like little devils but the ladies refused saying it just wasn't "appropriate." The boys' mothers were thankful because they knew that boys who look like the devil are too easily tempted to act like the devil. Many kids wanted cat faces and most wanted ferocious cat faces so they could look like little Howlers. The ladies were ready for that but, as the Howler faces left the booth, most of them were issuing loud howling sounds of many kinds.

Another new thing this year was the arrival of three farmers each driving a wagon loaded with tables, chairs, and all sorts of Melons and fresh fruits. A big sign declared that their area at the end of the street was now the Melon Patch Café. Selling only fresh fruit, melons, and lemonade, the attraction was a very popular place for older people to "sit a spell" and relax during the day.

By nine o'clock the streets were beginning to fill with curious children being trailed by their families and Margie and Maggie at the Two Sisters Café were serving a huge crowd at their outdoor tables. A sign advertised that by noon they would be selling Billy Burgers, a special ground beef sandwich creation just for Howler Days. By 9:30 the first band arrived. They played on the courthouse lawn and called themselves a "fiddle band" but that wasn't quite accurate because four of the men and boys played fiddles but two of them played string basses that they called "bull fiddles."

At 10:00 sharp the crowd moved toward the bandstand where the talent contest was scheduled. Several people competed in three categories. Some were very good and some were really not. The three categories were "singers, players, and others." The players were people who performed on musical instruments and the singers of course sang songs. The most popular performers were in the "other" group. They included comedians, jugglers, acrobats, and story-tellers. One young man from the college in Rolla rode on a dangerous-looking contraption called a "bicycle." It had one gigantic wheel on the front and a tiny wheel on the back.

Billy was fascinated by two of the story tellers who told wild tales in the most exaggerated style. Billy kept looking around at all of the people in the audience as they laughed, moaned, and applauded the wild claims of the storytellers. Watching Billy that day was like watching a good baseball player who was seeing his first major league game.

I don't think I've told you this yet but I used to have a problem when I talked. It was something called a speech impediment. I used to feel that everyone was staring at me when I talked and I just hated to say anything in front of a bunch of people. One thing I immediately liked about Billy was that my impediment didn't seem to matter to him at all. In fact, he acted like he didn't even notice it. But my impediment made me admire Billy even more when he would tell stories or talk to a big crowd like he was going to do again today.

When the contest was over and the prizes were awarded to winners the Mayor made a short speech welcoming everyone and reminding them of all the good things in the town that day and every day. Then people began to clear the bandstand to make room for the brass band which was next on the schedule. At that time Billy stayed in the booth with Mary Jean to sign and sell her art work. I just wandered through the town seeing what was new this year. I had a few cents in my pocket but I wasn't going to spend anything until I had seen everything.

As I walked I noticed a group of four boys about my age leaning against a hitching rail. I didn't know them but I do remember that they looked different than anyone else in town because they weren't going anywhere and they weren't smiling. I thought to myself, "Those boys are up to something," and I remembered the spectacle of the skunks at last year's festival.

No one knew who might have released those skunks or even if they were released at all. It could be that the skunks just wandered into town after being attracted by the aromas of the food. But, in fact, these were the very same boys and they were still jealous of Billy Bob getting all the attention. And, once again, they had something terrible planned.

****

At exactly two o'clock the Mayor was scheduled to speak and after a few minutes, he was to introduce the town's hero, Billy Bob Caldwell. This year I had been in on the adventure so I was asked to be there also. I suppose those four boys didn't know about that but it did put me right next to the stage so I could see most of what happened. I was nervous about the whole thing so I waited with Billy in Mary Jean's booth while he autographed a few more drawings. We looked up to see that the Mayor was waiting for us. He motioned for us to join him and he seemed impatient.

We went over to the bandstand and I stood next to the steps while Billy went on up to join the Mayor. Just before we got there a boy must have arrived with two bowls of beef stew from one of the vendors across the street. A note said that one was for the Mayor and one was for Billy. "They probably want us to say something about how good it is," the Mayor told Billy. Since he was supposed to speak first, he ate his down really fast and then got up to talk. The crowd pressed close around to hear the Mayor and Billy stood at the back eating his bowl of stew. He finished it and then looked over at me and made a sour face. He apparently didn't think the stew tasted very good.

We found out later that the four boys I had seen had bought the stew and gave it to Billy and the Mayor. As they carried the bowls across the street, they added something to each bowl called ipecac syrup. It's what people take if they accidentally eat something that's poison. It gets the poison food out of your stomach. That's right ipecac syrup makes people throw up.

Some folks will tell you that the Mayor is "full of himself" and loves to be in the spotlight but everyone had to admit that day that he was a courageous person too. As he greeted the throng of people, his stomach began to make loud noises like something between a gurgle and a roar. I was standing at the side of the bandstand and I could hear it so I'm sure the people closer to him could hear it too. He knew he was in trouble and had to get away from the crowd as fast as he could so he began to talk very rapidly.

People in the crowd realized that something was wrong and they looked at each other and then began to press even closer to get a better look at the mayor. They also came closer because by this time he wasn't speaking loudly any more. He began to look funny also as his mouth became more round and he kept his lips close together. I heard one little girl say, "Look, Mommy, the funny Mayor went to the face painting booth and they made him all green!"

The Mayor mumbled something like, "Ladies and Gentlemen, I give you our hero, Billy Bob mmmpphhhh mmmpphhh......." With this he ran for the steps and actually bumped me as he flew down the steps and around to the back of the bandstand and fell to his hands and knees where no one could see him. As the stew exploded out, the sight was ugly and the smell was even worse.

Now Billy had eaten his stew also but just a couple of minutes later. He was already holding his stomach when he stepped forward to speak. I looked at Mary Jean and she also knew that something was terribly wrong. Billy was truly a tough kid but he looked like he was about to cry and the people applauded and cheered for him. He waited as long as he could but then turned and ran toward the back rail of the bandstand. Neither he nor the crowd had any way of knowing that the Mayor was kneeling back there.

Like a seasick passenger on a ship, Billy shot the entire stinking contents of his stomach over the railing and out through the air. The Mayor heard it happen and looked up just in time to see the shower of vomit falling like chunky rain onto him and his new suit and hat. When Billy opened his eyes he beheld the angriest person he had ever seen in his life.

Luckily the Mayor's anger turned toward the perpetrators. "Find him!" He yelled at the Sheriff. "Find whoever did this! He'll wish he had never been born!" With that the Mayor went running for home and a bath.

Billy's mother was a teacher and she knew how to handle emergencies. She was on the bandstand immediately and swept Billy away to clean his face and find out what had happened. But the ordeal was not over for either Billy or the Mayor. They weren't able to be seen in public for several hours.

Rev. Caldwell was helped by two men and he managed to get up into the bandstand and then he called for me to join him. "I'm very sorry, Ladies and Gentlemen," he said. "I have no idea what just happened. At least I have no idea why that just happened. But I know that most of you came to this spot to hear what Billy had to say about his latest adventure. It just happens that there were two other people on that adventure and we are still here. So why don't we just make this a question and answer time and we'll try to tell you everything you want to know."

I'll have to admit that the people of Flanders weren't as polite that day as usual. Everyone kept talking to each other and trading stories as they tried to figure out exactly what had happened.

Crime and Punishment

As Rev. Caldwell and I talked, I could see the entire crowd including the four boys across the street. But now they had changed. Before, they were conspicuous because they weren't smiling. Now they were conspicuous because they were holding their stomachs and belly-laughing. They were even laughing so hard that they had to wipe tears from their eyes.

I saw a deputy sheriff and called him to the back of the bandstand while Billy's dad continued to answer questions. I told the deputy to check on those four boys and he did immediately. In minutes a group of men led by the deputy were taking the four boys down the street in the direction of the Sheriff's Office next to the Courthouse.

I hurried to the Sheriff's Office as soon as I could. Luckily, I got there in time to see some interesting things happen. First, the deputy had the boys turn their pockets inside-out and one had an empty ipecac bottle. One of the adults left to get Mr. Medley at the drug store. When he arrived they asked him what ipecac was and he explained that it was something used to induce vomiting. All eyes turned toward the boys and they seemed to be trying to shrink into the woodwork.

Mr. Medley stated that the boys had been in his store that morning and three of them made a commotion and distracted him while the other boy was on the opposite side of the store. "They left without buying anything," Mr. Medly added.

The deputy looked at the boy who had the bottle, "Son, I hope you have a paid receipt for that bottle."

The boys just stood there having nothing at all to say. "I don't know what kind of charges might be filed," the deputy said, "but theft for sure. I'm going to have to lock you up until someone comes to claim you."

****

Several hours went by before I saw an elderly lady go into the Sheriff's Office. By that time Billy was doing better and so was the Mayor. I went with Billy and the Mayor and the Sheriff to see who this woman was. She turned out to be the grandmother of two of the boys. "I came to get the boys," she said. "Their pappy won't come so he sent me."

"I wonder why he won't come," the Sheriff said. "Do you suppose he might be wanted for some crime himself?"

"No. It ain't nothin' like that," the woman answered. "He just makes some shine from time to time and he don't want to have no brush-up with the law."

"So let me get this straight," the Sheriff thought out loud. "The boys are accused of stealing and I'm supposed to keep them in jail until a parent comes to claim them. But the jail is no place for young boys – especially on a Saturday night."

He looked at the Mayor and then right into the woman's eyes and said, "I think I could get by with deputizing you for twenty-four hours and releasing the boys into your custody. But I'll only do that if you promise to make all their pappies come and talk to me. So, here's my offer. You take an oath as a temporary deputy and another oath that you will have these boys and their fathers attend tomorrow morning's community church service. After the service I'll talk with the boys' parents and we'll work something out. Will you have everyone there at 11:00 for church?"

"Sheriff, these boys done somthin' bad but we ain't bad people. I'll have every one of them there at 11:00 if I have to drag 'em by their ears."

With that the Sheriff nodded his head. He made her repeat an oath after him and the lady took the four boys and left. Billy Bob asked, "Sheriff, is there really such-of-a-thing as a temporary deputy?"

He looked at us and tried to look terribly serious. Then he held his right hand up and said, "Maybe."

The Mayor smiled at the Sheriff and said, "I know you. You're up to something!"

****

Sure enough the lady had a group of adults and the four boys at the church service just as she had promised. Immediately after the service most people left to find something good for lunch. Billy and I stayed to watch as the Sheriff and Mayor met with the little group to talk about what had happened. Soon, everyone shook hands and left. I think one of the men had given the Sheriff a coin and he took it straight to Mr. Medley's drug store.

I learned a few days later that on Monday the Sheriff had driven a wagon out to where the two brothers lived. He must have dynamited the big copper still that their father had been operating. Then the Sheriff returned to town with the boys' father and on the wagon was what was left of a copper boiler and tubing witch the man sold for scrap metal.

My father pointed out that Sheriffs are elected by the people and they have to handle situations in ways that satisfy the most people and still satisfy the law. "Sometimes that's a very hard thing to do," he said.

In this situation, the boys were caught, shamed, and warned. Mr. Medley was paid for his medication. The illegal still was destroyed and the moonshiner had the money from the copper he sold. Everyone was happy. Well, except the Mayor was still upset but he never let anyone know that. When people would laugh about the events of that day, he just tried to chuckle along with them.

My Favorite Place

If anyone were to ask me what was my favorite place I ever lived I wouldn't have to think about it for a second. Without a doubt, I loved living in Flanders. I liked the people, I liked the frontier life, I liked the school and church. Most important I liked my best friend, Billy Caldwell. I never actually had a brother or a sister but Billy sure seemed like family.

I was thinking about that one late afternoon in August. It was hot and humid and I was walking slowly. I even jumped into one farm pond on the way home – clothes and all. Of course I did take my shoes off. My parents would skin me if I didn't. I had to worry about it though because as soon as I put them back on, the water from my wet clothes and my socks made the shoes soaking wet too. "Next time I'll have to be sure and go barefoot until I dry off," I thought.

Sadly, when I got home, I didn't give a hoot about my shoes and neither did my parents. They tried to act happy but I think they were really feeling the same way that I did. I was fourteen years old then but I skipped dinner and went to bed where I cried like a baby. I cried most of the night until I finally fell asleep to have terrible dreams.

****

The next day I went to Billy's house to talk with him. His father answered the door and told me that Billy was waiting for me at the clubhouse. When I got there Billy was all excited and ran to meet me. "I found a bunch of big ones!" he said. "Those frogs are all grown up and

I found a whole passel of big ones just downstream from the clubhouse. Come on and get a gig. We're gonna eat well today!

He stopped and looked at me and knew something was wrong but I decided right on the spot not to tell him what it was. "Let's go ahead and have a good day," I thought. "Billy's so excited and I don't want to spoil it for him." I thought that maybe his parents knew the news and had already told it to him but he seemed to have no idea at all.

We gigged frogs and had good luck even in the bright daylight. But for hungry boys, the legs even of big frogs, aren't very filling so we put some fishing lines into the water also. By lunchtime we had a bucket of frogs and a good string of fish. We kept an iron skillet at the clubhouse and Billy had brought a small tub of lard so we built a small fire and seasoned the skillet while we cleaned the frogs and fish. The leftover parts went into the river to feed the fish that we would have for the next meal. Then it hit me that there might not be a next meal.

The fish were cleaned and split so we decided to cook them Indian-style. We put green sticks in the split and propped the fish open so heat from the coals would roast the flesh completely through. While these slowly baked we took out our pocket knives and sliced up the potatoes that Billy had brought from his garden. They went into the lard first and were soon spattering and sending up a wonderful aroma.

When the potatoes were just starting to get brown and crusty, we put the frog legs in with them and let the two foods finish cooking together. We sat and watched in fascination as the frog legs jerked and jumped around in the skillet. No matter how many times we might have seen it, jumping frog legs always fascinated us.

That was a wonderful moment that I will always treasure. Sitting with my best friend at a small campfire with potatoes and frog legs cooking and sending up just enough smoke to make us even hungrier than we would otherwise be. The fish resting on green sticks above the coals dripped little bits of fish oil onto the coals once in a while and each time it sent little puffs of steamy smoke into the air. This contributed another aroma to the smell of the wood fire, the potatoes, the frog legs, and the lard itself. The water in the river giggled musically over the stones and the leaves in the tops of the trees rustled an accompaniment each time the breeze would blow. The fire snapped and popped the percussion for the little symphony. Could life ever be better than this?

When the frog legs and potatoes were both brown and crusty, we divided them onto two large leaves that we used for plates. We burned our fingers and tongues on the hot delicacies but it was worth the minor pain. The feast was complete as we shared the flakey white fish. Then we both leaned back and complained about having eaten too much. Could life ever be better than this?

We talked all the rest of the day about plans for the future and about what high school would be like. As we walked through the woods trying to find animal tracks we talked about the boys who set the skunks loose and doctored the stew. "Would they be at our high school?" we wondered. We talked a little about what came after high school but that seemed so far away that it was just too hard to imagine.

Billy confessed that he was really impressed by the storytellers at Howler Days and that someday, just for a hobby maybe, he might like to be a storyteller. I told him that I suspected he already was a storyteller. He seemed to like that. "What do you want to do for just for fun?" he asked me. I told him that I hoped to learn to play a musical instrument but I'd be pretty happy to just go fishing from time to time.

Late in the afternoon the sunshine gave way to thin gray clouds and those became thicker and darker before a drizzly rain began to fall. We went back to the clubhouse and took one wall down so we could move the fire a little closer. Once we had the fire closer to us, we sat under the roof and listened to the gentle rain all around. It was very peaceful and we sat without talking for a long time. Finally, I told Billy the news.

"Billy," I said quietly, "my dad's company is transferring him to another town. It's called Maryville and it's way up by Iowa and Nebraska."

He sat there with disbelief in his eyes. "How far away is that?" he wanted to know.

"Hundreds of miles," I answered.

****

The next day Billy came to my house. That was a little unusual because I had no river or hiking trails at my home. The clubhouse, fishing, and everything else we enjoyed together were at Billy's place. Even more unusual was that he was there shortly after the sun came up. I was still feeding the chickens and giving them fresh water when I heard someone knocking at the front door. I was very surprised to walk around the house and see Billy on the front porch talking to my mother. He motioned for me to come up to the porch and my mother told Billy and me to come in for breakfast.

Billy said that he had already eaten but he would sit with us and maybe have a glass of milk. We washed up and when my father arrived we all sat around the kitchen table and I think we were all a little sad except for

Billy. Billy, on the other hand, was cheerful and looked like he was about to spring one of his stories on us. He may have eaten already but he ate as much as anyone else as we sat there together.

Finally the meal was finished and Billy said, "I've got this thing all figured out!"

"I think you might need to explain it to us," my father said. "What thing are you talking about?" Of course we knew that he meant the move to Maryville.

"Well," he began, "when you folks move to Maryville, Roger can stay here and live with my family. Everybody already thinks he's my brother anyway!"

Without thinking I blurted out, "Yeah! Can I stay and live with Billy?"

My mother's eyes teared up and she said, "Honey, we love you. We'd be lost without you. We're a family. Wouldn't you miss us?"

Of course she was right. I could never feel good about living hundreds of miles from my parents. "Maybe Billy could go to Maryville with us," I suggested but I knew that was a stupid idea.

Billy said, "My family really needs me now – especially my dad."

"And Mary Jean really needs you," I said in a sweet exaggerated voice. My parents didn't know whether to laugh or not but Billy and I sure did. We could always joke and make fun of each other. Brothers are like that.

We sat for a while with no one saying anything. At one point I asked, "Are there any trains between Maryville and Flanders?"

My father said that a person could go to St. Joseph and get on a train to Hannibal and then at Hannibal get on another train to St. Louis.

Then he would have to find another train to Rolla and Flanders. Or maybe the person could go all the way to Kansas City and get a train to Springfield and then go east to Rolla and Flanders. "Either way," my father said, "It's a terrible long journey that would take at least two days of travel and waiting in the terminals just to go one way on the trip. Then it would be that far to get back home again."

We sat again for a long time with no one saying anything. I knew that my dad was late for work but he understood how important this was. I appreciated the way they let Billy sit at our table and be a part of the family for this important conversation. I didn't like what was happening but I fully realized what a good family I had and how lucky I was in many ways.

"Dad," I said, "do you have to work for that company? Or if you do, does that mean that we have to move so often? I mean couldn't you just run the company's office here in Flanders for a few more years?"

I could tell that my dad was thinking very carefully and finally he said, "Roger, I know how you and Billy love to explore the woods and have adventures. Sometimes I wish I could be there too. I never got to do that when I was a boy. But now, I'm like a pioneer or an explorer in the business world. When we go to a new town it's because my company has never been there before. I start a business that has never been there before and I meet people who never heard of my company. Every place we go is like a new frontier for me and I'm a pioneer. That's what I'm really good at doing and that's why I'm so valuable to my company. It's why they pay me so well."

"I love my job, Roger. I love what I do every day and I already know that I'm going to love getting started in Maryville. As far as that goes, I'll bet that you'll learn to love living in Maryville too. And remember, you have four years of high school and then you'll be on your own. You can move back and live in Flanders if you want."

Billy and I looked at each other and knew that in four years we wouldn't be boys any more. Everything would probably be different in four years. "Billy will be married by then," I said and we smiled at each other. But his was a sad smile and probably mine was too. We knew the best year of our lives was just about over.

Conclusion

Billy went on home that morning and we didn't get together again that day. The next morning I walked out to Billy's house and his parents were especially nice to me. They gave Billy and me some especially nice food to take with us for the day's adventure and said that he didn't have to do the chores that day. We walked toward the river and talked a little but it wasn't fun. I went home early and ate lunch with my mother.

The high school opened that Wednesday – not for classes but for business and for an open house. I went for curiosity and to get my records to take to Maryville High School. Mrs. Caldwell had sent the records on to the Flanders High School last May but now they didn't need them and I did.

While I was waiting in the office for my folder Mary Jean saw me and came in to say hello. She decided to wait and when I was ready she took me out to meet some of the other kids. After a while she said, "Do you believe me now? I told you that there are lots of pretty girls in the school and nice ones at that. I told you that there would be lots of girls who would be interested in you. Do you believe me now?"

It was true. Several very nice and very pretty girls had been especially friendly so to answer Mary Jean's question, I just smiled and nodded my head. She stopped me and stepped around right in front of me. "Listen," she said, "I'm pretty sure the girls here, and the boys too, are just about the same as those in Maryville. You're a very nice guy and not bad looking. I think you're going to love high school in Maryville."

"Hey, Roger," a voice said from behind, "if you meet any real sweethearts in Maryville will you let me know. There's not much to choose from here. I mean these girls are so bossy! And there all so ugly they could scare the fleas off a hound dog!"

Of course it was Billy and I promised to report to him about the girl situation in Maryville. "Don't give him any ideas," Mary Jean told me. She grabbed Billy's arm and took him away from me and my ideas about Maryville girls.

I was leaving school when I saw another familiar face. One of the skunk & ipecac boys was there at the high school. I wondered what words might pass between Billy and that boy when they met.

Walking home, I went slowly and looked at everything I wanted to remember about my favorite town. My mother was trying to be pleasant and cheerful but it was just an act. Still, though I appreciated that she was trying to make things better for me. I gave her the folder of records from the school and went to my room to do some more packing.

Billy stopped on his way home and we tried to talk but neither of us felt like saying too much. We promised that we would write each other but we both knew that wouldn't last. It just wasn't our style. We decided to ask our parents if we could each spend a month at the other's house in the summer. We did ask but I don't remember what was said about it. I just know that I never saw Billy again.

****

Billy and I did write to each other a few times. He told me that after graduating, Mary Jean went off to School at Stephens College in Columbia. She would study art. She promised to write to him all that year and the next year Billy could go to the University of Missouri in Columbia so he could be close to Mary Jean. I think he said he wanted to study Wildlife Conservation. I learned years later that after college they got married in a small wedding but no one other than family was invited.

I liked high school in Maryville and made good friends there. When I graduated, I went to William Jewel College in Liberty and studied to be a teacher. That's why today I'm teaching eighth grade and trying to be as good as my eighth grade teacher back in Flanders.

****

Now, don't get the wrong idea. I don't think this story is over quite yet. At least I hope it's not. You see, I got busy one time and went looking through the library for some news about Billy Bob and what might have become of him. I was not surprised at all to find a number of books written by a man named William R. Caldwell and I remembered that Billy's middle name was really Robert. "This might be my old friend," I thought. He always was a story teller.

Then I saw the titles of the books. There was one named *Booger Dogs* and another was *Aquatic Giants in Midwestern Rivers*. He wrote one about *The Gift for Water Witching*, and another about *The Joplin Spook Light*. Who else but Billy Bob Caldwell would write books about subjects like that? It just had to be my old friend!

I also read that next Saturday the Greene County Library is sponsoring one of their "Conversations with the Experts" where the subject is "Hoop Snakes – Reality or Fiction." They advertise that their special guest is the author, William R. Caldwell. I'm planning to drive to

Springfield for that. Do you think Billy Bob will remember his friend from so long ago?

Author's Note

When I wrote this story I got some of my ideas from history, some from Missouri's maps and some from the old school picture that you see below. Can't you just imagine the boy on the left being full of stories and having a wild imagination. Can't you look at his eyes and think he's full of mischief. If he was old enough to be an eighth-grader, he could be Billy Bob. The boy on the right looks like a boy who would love to tag along and be impressed by Billy, doesn't he? Well, that could have been a description of me when I was in school.

And it just happens that the two boys look very much like my best friend and me when we were in school. That's how I got the feel for the boys, their friendship, and their adventures.

And what about the Ozarks Howler? When Ms. Blake did the drawing that you see on the front cover of this book, her job was easy in a way. You see no one can tell you exactly what a Howler looks like.

There is no one who has ever seen one and is alive to tell about it. Some people years ago wrote descriptions of the Howler but those descriptions didn't always match each other. Ms. Blake got to draw what she thinks the descriptions mean.

Did you notice that every time the newspaper editor reported a story about the Howler, he let the readers' imaginations believe in the big cat. He sort of led the readers to believe what he wanted them to. Why do you think he did that? Do you think that people reporting the news today might present the news in such a way that it makes you want to buy their newspaper or watch their TV reporting?

And what about Mayor Wellman? He started out angry about Billy Bob's stories. But soon he was promoting the stories and introducing Billy to the world as a hero. Why do you suppose he changed his mind? Of course it was pretty much the same reason as the newspaper editor.

There is one part of this story that probably could not have been true. Married women were usually not allowed to teach at public schools in those days. I'm sure that there were some places on the frontier where the only available teachers were married women like Billy's mother so the little school might hire them until they could find a man or a single woman. It wasn't until 1944 when cities like St. Louis and Kansas City first allowed women to continue teaching after they were married. That, of course, was because of the great shortage of teachers caused by the World War.

Billy's father suffered a terrible consequence from a cut on his leg which became infected. It was called gangrene. The old doctor in Ironton had seen many cases of gangrene from soldiers' wounds and had amputated many limbs because of it. Did you know that gangrene is still a problem today. Now it usually doesn't happen because of a wound but because of poor blood circulation. Exercise is probably the best way to prevent gangrene from ever bothering you.

It may seem hard for today's readers to understand just how isolated those small towns in the Ozarks were more than a hundred years ago. The railroad changed that but only for the towns along the line. If you want to understand just how much of an isolated frontier wilderness the area south of Rolla was in those days, it's pretty easy to do. Much of that part of Missouri is still the Mark Twain National Forest and much of the river system in that part of the state is today called the National Scenic Riverways so it is still very natural and still very much of a wilderness.

You can experience some of that wilderness feeling these days by taking a float trip on the Current, the Jack's Fork, the Huzzah, the Meramec, or any of the other rivers in the region. There are some roads made by more modern people but they are so curvy that the local people say when you drive your car there, you can sometimes see your own taillights. Still today, people in the Ozarks like to tell stories, don't they?

Even now, in the twenty-first century, that part of the state is populated by elk, black bears, mountain lions, and other animals that have long ago disappeared from the more developed areas. And many kinds of fish inhabit the rivers just as they have for thousands of years.

Music has always been an important part of life in the Ozarks but it was almost always singing and string instruments. At about the time that Billy Bob and Roger were boys, the brass instruments were being introduced and were becoming popular in rural communities. You had to have enough wealthy people to be able to purchase brass instruments so a brass band was something any community would be proud of. Since it was fairly new to most rural people, being in a brass band then was a lot like being in a rock band now.

Do you remember when the boys tied a young tree over with a leather thong and used it for bouncing up and down? Kids have been doing that in the Ozarks for hundreds and maybe thousands of years. We know that some of those trees called "thong trees" are way too old to have been done by white settlers so the Native Americans must have been the ones to tie them over. Of course we don't know exactly why they did it.

This is a thong tree that is still pretty young.

After the tree was bent over it still wanted to grow toward the sunlight so it turned itself back upward giving us this unusual shape today. Some that the Osage tied are now huge and well over a hundred years old but they still have this distinctive shape.

Do you remember Roger describing that new invention, the bicycle? They still weren't well-known in the Ozarks at this time, mostly because there weren't many good places to ride. The roads were just long strips of dirt or mud. They were often covered with horse manure. Farmers still drove their herds and flocks of chickens, turkeys, pigs, and cattle down the dirt roads. When you rode your bike through the mud or the manure, some would stick to the wheel and come flying up onto the rider.

This early kind of bike is called a high wheel bicycle. The idea of the large wheel was to help it go across bumps and holes in the road. However, if it didn't go easily across a pothole the rider would be thrown over the front wheel and onto the road. Mark Twain used to ride this kind of bicycle and he described his experience:

> *"I didn't always go over the front way; I had other ways, and practiced them all; but no matter which way was chosen for me there was always one monotonous result --- the bicycle skinned my leg and leaped up into the air and came down on top of me."*

He went on to say, "

> *After a day's practice, I arrived at home with my skin hanging in ribbons, from my knees down. It was always a surprise to me that I had so much skin, and that it held out so well. There was always plenty, and I soon came to understand that the supply was going to remain sufficient for all my needs.'*

Just for fun, take a good look at that picture and try to figure out how you would get up and onto the bicycle.

Some people who read this story will realize that there is a strong comparison to a true story that happened up by Louisiana, Missouri. MoMo, the Missouri Monster was spotted in 23 counties and was described by all sorts of people. He smelled terrible, looked ugly, and ate people's dogs. A local radio station broadcaster wrote a song about the monster and the local merchants still have a big celebration each year in honor of the creature. They named a ride for MoMo at the Six Flags theme park near St. Louis and a desert was named for MoMo at a popular eatery in St. Louis. All of this in spite of the fact that it turned out to be some boys with a fake fur coat who wanted to scare some girls from their school. People really like to be scared. It's fun!

Now I'll answer the big question. I know that about 50% of the boys who read this book want to know more about ipecac syrup and where they can get their hands on some. Ipecac syrup was discovered by some Native South Americans who made a similar substance from the root of an ipecac tree. For hundreds of years people in Europe and America used it whenever someone (like a young child) might accidentally swallow poison or someone else's medicine. It made the person vomit and therefore brought up the poison and got it out of the stomach.

However, it turns out that, while it does make people throw up, it doesn't do a very good job of getting out the bad stuff. So they no longer make or sell ipecac in any stores. Sorry!

It's a little bit unusual that Roger recognized right at the time that the year he spent in Flanders was the best year of his life. Too often we don't appreciate what we have at any point in time. We later look back at our life and realize just how good things were at certain times. We should always try to appreciate and cherish what we have when we have it. He might have also been unaware of many good things still to come in his life. For instance, many people will say that the best time of their life was during high school or college. Others say it was when their children or their grandchildren are growing up. Life is holding all sorts of good things for us that we can never anticipate.

I hope you enjoyed spending this year with Billy and Roger and all of the good people who lived in the Ozarks more than a hundred years ago. Some of their children have moved away to find more opportunities but some of the smart ones appreciate what they have and are still here in this beautiful place.